GOOD COMPANY

For Tony Cook –
wordsmith and
seeker of blue skys.

best,
Doug 11/07

GOOD COMPANY

Douglas A. Harper

THE UNIVERSITY OF CHICAGO PRESS

Chicago and London

The University of Chicago Press, Chicago 60637
The University of Chicago Press, Ltd., London

89 88 87 86 85 84 83 82   5 4 3 2 1

Library of Congress Cataloging in Publication Data

Harper, Douglas A.
  Good company.

  Bibliography: p.
  1. Tramps—United States.   I. Title.
HV4505.H37   305.5′6   81–11367
ISBN 0–226–31686–6   AACR2

Douglas A. Harper is assistant professor of sociology
at State University College, Potsdam, New York.

The design stamped on the front cover is a tramp sign
meaning "Hit the road, quick!"

For my mother and father

Contents

Acknowledg- ments

I owe very much to many, for their encouragement, their prodding and their criticism. Everett Hughes, Irv Zola and Charlie Fisher guided a different version of this book through the Brandeis sociology department as a doctoral dissertation. While all shared the responsibilities of dissertation advisers (defined at Brandeis in personal as well as academic terms) I experienced a particular joy and honor as the student of Everett Hughes.

G. I. Schaffner and Toni Johnson were involved from the very beginning, reading numerous drafts and offering a steady stream of criticism and support. This has been a clear case of the exploitation of dear friends. Earl Ostroff and Jim Spradley read the first draft and made helpful suggestions. Upton Brady of the Atlantic Monthly Press was very helpful in the long process of shaping a book from a dissertation. Howard S. Becker and Jonathan Imber offered particularly important suggestions for revisions of the last chapter. Finally, Bruce Jackson became a thorn in my side at a point when I was about ready to let the book die after the third revision which hadn't yet worked. Jackson became the most important kind of mentor, absolutely unsparing in his criticism but willing to read and reread, always pointing to places that needed more and more and more work. There is no way to pay this kind of debt. It has to be the central relationship in what we often idealize as the academic world, the relationship in which the spirit as well as the form of this peculiar seeking is passed along.

Other kinds of debts are owed. The work from which this book derived came from a life that was interwoven with others. Steven Scoll, Gregory John Prang, G. I. Schaffner and Jesse Johnson shared experiences that preceded and followed what I've described in this manuscript. Lee Lord and Missy Allen offered help of the most important kind and Kate Kennedy provided a western respite from what at times became a hard road. Suzan integrated the final revisions into our life together, taking care of our son, Colter, for much of two summers while final revisions were completed.

Betty Wells skillfully and patiently copyedited and typed at least three drafts and remained cheerful throughout. My thanks to all of the above, and many more I have not mentioned. In one way or another they've all been good company.

GOOD COMPANY

Prologue

I was drinking beer with some tramps one night in the fall of 1973. Jack and Eddie had buddied up when Jack picked Eddie "out of the gutter" in Wenatchee, and he'd taken him along to a job he'd arranged picking apples. Jack had an old car and called himself a rubber tramp. Eddie didn't say much and he didn't work very hard. He looked old and worn out but Jack had an interest in him for some reason and was always saying things like: "Now Eddie, you aren't going off to drink that old wine no more, now are you?" And Eddie would shake his head back and forth—he wasn't going back; he wasn't going back.

I didn't know how they'd ended up together, but I thought that they must have known each other someplace down the road. Jack was talking about the times he'd had: jobs, cars, drunks, bad rides, when Eddie interrupted: "Last job *I* had was making brooms for fourteen cents an hour—made two-hundred-forty dollars in sixteen months."

Jack banged his beer down on the table and stared at the other tramp: "Two-hundred-forty in sixteen months? You been on the *inside*?"

The tramp looked like he'd wished he'd kept his mouth shut. He finally nodded and started telling us about twenty years behind the bars of San Quentin, Alcatraz, and other prisons I'd never heard of. Jack kept looking at him like he couldn't believe his ears, and I was a little surprised the subject hadn't come up in the month they'd been together. Jack finally asked him what he'd done to get himself in so much trouble and the tramp said: "It's checks—always little chickenshit checks. My problem is my education—I know how to write my name. Did you ever think of it? Just sign your name and they give you money. It never fails to amaze me to find out my name's still good after all the trouble I've been in."

Jack shook his head and looked away: "You must have liked it in there to keep going back."

"You don't know what you're talking about," Eddie shot back.

"If you didn't like it, why did you keep going back?"

1

"I ain't been in for two years, and I ain't going back," Eddie said.

Then Jack cooled off and told Eddie he thought he'd turned a corner. "You know what your problem is? You got to choose the right company. You got to choose the right company for a change—you gotta stay away from those goddam *skid* rows. How many times you been rolled on *skid* row?"

"Pretty near every time."

"You got to learn to choose your company better," Jack repeated slowly.

Eddie took a long pull from his beer, looked hard around the room and said: "That's something I been thinking about one hell of a lot these past twenty-three years—just who *is* good company?"

1

I'd been waiting for a train a year before in the same yard heading in the same direction but nothing seemed particularly familiar. The Minneapolis Burlington Northern yards stretch northwest from under the university and they go on for miles; ten, fifteen, twenty tracks wide; spurs heading north, spurs heading east; and somewhere in the maze a main line that carries the hotshot out of Chicago through Minneapolis to the west. I stood in the shadows of huge grain elevators, out of sight of the control tower, and I waited for a train due at midnight.

I'd been in the yards a couple of days, peeking around, asking questions and making plans. Every time I've gone back to the freights I've had to cross an emotional hurdle—they seem too big, too fast, too dangerous and too illegal—and I get used to the idea by spending a few days in the yards, testing the waters. If the brakemen aren't busy they'll answer a carefully worded question. If there are railroad police around it's better to encounter them just hanging around; no gear and no suspicious behavior. But then you choose the day: *tomorrow* you'll catch out, tonight you'll party and pack your gear and tomorrow you'll be back on the road. Then when you walk past the No Trespassing signs into the yard your traveling clothes and your gear mark you clearly. You enter a world that has its own rules and few second chances, and you'd better know what you're up to.

I was shifting back into a tramp world for the fourth or fifth time. I'd made cross country trips on freights and I'd spent some weeks the winter before living on Boston's skid row. These experiences were trips into a life I ordinarily did not lead, and I brought back from them photographs and scattered bits of writing. While my purpose was eventually to describe a tramp way of life my desire to record or document was only a part of the reason I'd go back again and again. The taste of camp coffee and the view from a flatcar on a slow ride through the Rockies were magnets that pulled hard indeed. This time I felt my gear in order and plans set. The Chicago hotshot would carry me across the Dakotas, Montana and the Rockies. As much as I had a

3

destination it was Wenatchee, Washington, for I knew it to be the center of the apple country and a junction of major rail lines. I knew the jungles in Wenatchee and I knew that there would be tramps there to steer me to a job. The Chicago hotshot, with the right connections, should get me to Wenatchee in no more than a couple of days. I mulled it over and relaxed. It seemed manageable, and it seemed in grasp.

After perhaps a half an hour the activity increased in the yard. Strings of boxcars were pushed up and down the parallel tracks, shuffled into boxcars, flatcars, gondolas and piggybacks that were being pushed uncoupled over the hump. The humped cars slammed into pieces of trains down one of the fifteen or twenty tracks that led away from the small hill and it was all controlled from a control tower that loomed above. The cars were shuffled and reshuffled; a few empties or badorders set off and pushed aside; a string of piggybacks or gondolas pushed into place—it went on and on like a carefully rehearsed play. I watched idly until I noticed a long string of empty grain cars and flat cars moving into place. I guessed that the grain cars would be going west, probably to Minot or Havre, and that the flats would go on to the lumbering country in the Rockies. As the train stretched out further and further I decided to find out.

I picked my way across the yard. It is with utmost care that one climbs over the couplings of boxcars for it is impossible to know when a car or engine will slam into it, compressing the long shaft on which the coupling is mounted and setting the car into a slow roll. The proper procedure is to throw one's gear over the couplings, then to climb across the space on the ladders and the braces on the car itself. It is quickly apparent in a freight yard that the scale is very unhuman—a small jolt to a freight car or a small compression of a coupling is enough to fling a person from the car and if you fall off climbing over you'll be run over or dragged down the yard. I moved over the couplings, first with hesitancy and then with more confidence as I found my "rail legs."

I found the longest section of train and began walking its length. I walked down the narrow canyon between the cars and came upon a tramp crouched near the door of the first empty boxcar. He did not see me coming and displeasure crossed his face when I suddenly appeared. He smelled of booze and sweat and urine and his work uniform looked like he'd slept in it for a week. His face was scarred and unshaven. He had some gear back in the boxcar so I asked him where he was headed. It was clear he wanted nothing to do with me but he answered that he was going west to pick apples. I told him that I too was going to Wenatchee to pick apples, but he answered, not a little sarcastically, that there wasn't any good work in *Wenatchee*, you had to go north, up the Okanagan to a place like Oroville. Before I could ask him where that was he'd slunk back to the corner of his car. I walked on to find my own.

I was nearly to the end of the train before I found another empty boxcar. It was old and battered, without wooden liners on the walls that would cool and quiet the ride. The wheels were mounted in old-style bearings that make an empty car jump and skitter and the floor was covered with strapping iron and sawdust. I did not like the car but it was the only inside ride on the train. I checked to see if it was a badorder on its way to a repair yard before I threw my gear in the door.

I found some cardboard sheets to make a mattress and pushed some of the litter out of the car. A brakeman stuck his head in the door and startled me but he seemed friendly and interested. He told me the train was due out on the highline—the old Great Northern tracks—as soon as it got its power. It would make the five-hundred mile run to Minot before breaking up and it should get me there a few hours before the hotshot which was still due at midnight, so I'd be able to catch a few hours sleep before continuing on. Then our conversation should have been over but he lingered. He told me he'd tramped all over the west when he was younger and he always tried to help a man out "as long as they looked like they knew what they were doing." It was all going down hill, he said; the tramps were bums and there were hippies on the trains always getting into trouble. You don't mind a rider, he repeated, if they know what they're doing. But the hippie will lie around in the open smoking dope as though it's a picnic, and then they'll get hurt and sue the railroad. He shook his head, muttered that the world was going to hell, and walked away.

As my car slammed back and forth I pegged the doors open with old brake linings and railroad spikes. The idea is to keep the doors from jolting shut as there is no way to open them from the inside. Ruined brakelines are lying around the yard and they can be banged

5

into the space between the door and the car, and even though they usually fall out after a few hours it is a job that is always done.

As I worked, a yard engine lumbered by, sounding like it was overrevving moving so slowly. Two green Burlington Northern engines, attached back to back, idled alongside and past my boxcar. I caught sight of the engineer and our eyes met briefly but his expression did not change. Just a minute later the air hissed down the brakelines and the highball whistle blew. I was filled with a lonely sort of expectancy—an intense desire to be underway. Then the engineer snapped the throttle back, the jolt crashed down the train and the trip began.

As the train pulled out of the yard and gained speed the memories came flooding back. The noise and movement are soon more than I've experienced. Nothing can be so loud! Nothing can throw me about with such abandon! The car, sprung for hundreds of tons, carries me as a tiny piece of flotsam bouncing, banging, swaying. The car rocks from side to side and I think of empty boxcars tipping and taking whole freight trains with them. You don't live through those, say the tramps. The car bangs so hard on road crossings I hold my mouth open to keep my teeth from cracking together. I try to sit and my body leaps off the floor and my sleeping bag skitters away. Slack creeps into the mile long train and as the car suddenly snaps ahead I find my body accomplishing the anatomical feat of moving three directions at once. I stand with my legs spread for balance holding a wall using my knees for shocks. The train highballs and the tracks are bad and my car rides worse than any I remember. Or perhaps it just seems this way every time I go back. The eight hours ahead seem interminable but the train does not slow to ease my aches.

I spend the hours standing by the door. When the tracks parallel a highway I catch a glimpse of car travelers safely encapsulated. Sometimes they wave but more often they look away and shield their children from the sight of me. An outlaw so soon! I laugh aloud but I cannot hear myself above the din of the train. I am captured by the absurdity. I run back and forth through the car; leap, play, dash about. I'm back on the road but the train moves on its own will. I'm a small grain attached but I'll remain. With all the swirling grit my trip is cleaner by far than those on the highway for there is no windshield constricting my view and no billboards to funnel my attention. I feel the land, standing quite near, and it becomes very much a part of my trip.

I pass through time as the train slices through pink and avocado subdivisions; belts of older, taller and more muted houses; and finally through stone-facaded sections of the towns. The train depots were the centers, the kernels from which these towns grew, but now only an old trainman stands on the platform and waves as the freight high-balls through.

We pass for an hour through an area dotted with lakes before entering the Red River valley. The transformation is quick and complete. Fields of sunflowers stretch to the horizon; then comes quarter section after quarter section of corn with farm buildings and houses tucked into small tree-filled corners and straight and regular roads tying it all together.

Well into the evening the train slowed for the first time to a fifteen-mile-an-hour idle through the Fargo/Moorhead yards and I watched ten or twelve tramps waiting to board. They stayed away from my car and I was glad to be left alone when the train pulled into the North Dakota prairie.

As the sun set, the train turned due west. I looked around the edge of the door and watched the mile long train bore directly into the orange sun on the horizon. It got dark fast and I became depressed, feeling quite isolated, separated and alone. I was nearly overcome with my tiredness before I crawled into my sleeping bag and went to sleep to the lurching, rocking, and screeching of my freight car.

I awoke startled; the train had stopped.

I heard footsteps and stumbled to my feet. The steps neared my car, then the beam of a flashlight bore into my eyes.

"We in Minot?" I called out, but the confidence in my voice was a mask for my fear.

"*Minot?*" He turned the flashlight away and walked on. "Naw, hell, this ain't Minot. Minot's two hundred miles north on the old Great Northern tracks. You're on the Northern Pacific, outside Bismarck."

"Where's this train headed?" I yelled, but he was already out of earshot. A few minutes later we were back on the road.

We changed crews during the stop and the new engineer seemed less interested in keeping the slack out of the couplings. The car would lurch ahead, then snap back. I fought my way back to sleep.

I awoke in the red light of dawn. I came jolting back to consciousness and my situation seemed improbable—a master trick I'd played once again on myself. I gathered my gear, strewn by the movement of the car, washed with canteen water, and ate.

The train sped along a cottonwood-bordered river still covered by an early morning mist. The land was wet with dew but the sky was clear. The pace seemed a bit slower and the rocking and bouncing was easier. We came to the town of Big Horn, and then Custer, and I figured out that the river along the tracks was the Yellowstone. I was in Montana, on the Northern Pacific line, and I expected the train would break up in Billings.

At noon we entered Billings but rolled through the yard and continued west. I thought I'd get another division out of the ride but fifteen miles down the track the train switched off the main line and entered a huge yard. It ground to a halt deep in the yard, with about twenty tracks of cars on either side. I decided to wait for a brakeman to find out if the train was breaking up or staying together and I missed the only westbound hotshot leaving that day. When I finally got the news I climbed through the cars, track after track, until I came to the edge of the yard just under the control tower. It was a hot Montana afternoon.

I walked over to an old black tramp reclining near the control tower on a stack of rotting pilings. He was a small man, dressed in dirty work clothes and a faded green hat. His gear was by his side: an old airlines bag and a hilex bottle of water. I dropped my gear on the ground near his, sat down and stretched in the sun.

I asked the tramp: "Do you know when there's a train heading toward Spokane?"

"There's going to be a bull local makin' up in a couple of hours. He's headed in that direction. Least that's what the braky told me. You just done and missed the hotshot."

"Hell, I been sitting on that one-eighty-two waiting to see if it was stayin' or leavin'," I said.

"You on that train, too? Where'd you come from?"

"Minneapolis. How about you?"

"Caught him in Fargo, right about sunset. Come to think of it, I mighta seen you."

"Did you ride an empty?"

"Naw, I hardly ever ride empties. Get throwed around too much. I ride gondolas—or piggybacks if it's rainin' or especially cold. I always get a heavy car, one that's carrying something."

"I guess that train we were riding left from Chicago. You ever ride back there?" I asked.

"I been through there, but it's hot. Hell, they'll *shoot* you if they as much as see you in the yards. You have to know where to catch your train, outside of the yards and on the run. The only time I been through there I was traveling streamlined and I was lucky . . .

"And they're mean out here, too, on the U.P., and even the Santa Fe. On the Santa Fe they have riding bulls. They ride in the crummy and jump the train at the edge of the yard to look for you. Like if we were sitting here in full view—hell, that'd catch us thirty days.

"You can ride that Union Pacific from Redding down to Southern California. You can ride him good all the way back to Salt Lake. Then he gets tough again. I've rode all over the northwest and I always made it. The only hot yards are those old U.P. yards in Portland, but you can beat those, too. They make up a train out of Spokane that don't even go into Pasco. He'll head down that bridge, and take you right into Portland. You just got to watch yourself and jump him outside the yards. There's a mean old bull sits in a shack at the edge of the yard . . ."

He paused and looked over to see if I was still listening.

"If you want a ride east, best way to catch him is in Hammond, south of Chicago. But you got to ride streamlined through there, too. It's hot. Then you ride 'im through to Fort Wayne, and into Buffalo. Takes you down to Hoboken, New Jersey. Only time I rode through there I was in a terrible fix. It was night and I was drunk, couldn't tell where I was and didn't much give a damn; ended up in Pennsylvania. It happened there in the Lackawanna freight yard, the front of the train broke off and took me all the way to Allentown, P-A—but the Lehigh Valley goes into Newark and I don't know if that yard is hot or not. But if you want to go to Newark go ahead and catch that Lehigh Valley, but jump him coming in. You'll be able to see the bull down the train, checking every car, so you get the hell out of there! You'll be all right.

"But you know, sometimes you can't hardly tell a bull. I walked up into a yard, on the Rock Island down there in Illinois, and the bull had a jacket on just like you have, only longer, and he had his gunbelt inside a pair of bib overalls. And his badge was on his belt buckle. Hell you'd walk right up on him. I did, as a matter of fact, and he told where to get the train!

"Now that bull in Minneapolis—he's been there twenty years. He'll never give you any trouble, except when that mail train comes through and then it's *damn* hot. They bring in federal people to watch that one. And they highball out of the yards so's you can't hardly grab him on the run. And they got travelin' bulls on that sonofabitch, too. I tried to ride him once, the goddamn bull run me off. They saw me get on and they stopped the whole goddamn train. Threw me off and watched so's I couldn't get back on. That was up in Havre . . .

"There's a bull in Yuma, Arizona, that'll run you out of the yard every time. But you can beat him, too. Just have to stay down past his shed and grab a piggyback—they're always running piggybacks—as he leaves the yard. Damn that bull gets mad! You can see him stomping around, getting meaner all the time!"

The old man paused.

"Just where is that train, and what is the Billings yard doing so far out of Billings?" I asked.

"This ain't the Billings yard; we're in Laurel. This is a main yard, and it's a big one. Billings is a small yard; most trains go right through. Now they got another yard, a little south, that used to be the Burlington yard before Burlington merged. So to get your hookups with Denver or Laramie you got to go through Billings—and head south. It's a big yard, so you got to be careful. But you can do it, and after you been through once you'll never forget how."

An hour passed. Over the din of clanging couplings and whirring yard engines the yard master in the control tower directed the making of the new train. The commands echoed back and forth through the yard like the disembodied voice of an announcer at a high school football game. We reclined in full view but were ignored.

Down the track to the west a figure carrying a bedroll, an aircraft bag, and a gallon hilex bottle of water hiked toward us. His pace was slow, his posture stooped, and dark blotches of sweat stained his khaki work shirt. As he approached, the black man asked: "Did that fella get on in Fargo? I thought I saw him in Fargo."

"No," I said. "I saw him in Minneapolis. Talked to him yesterday—unfriendly bastard." As the tramp approached I could see he looked the worse for wear from the thousand-mile trip. The sunlight highlighted the sores, the wrinkles and the grime that covered his body and gear. His first words were spat out: "Got one fucking dollar, walked all the way to town and it's Sunday. Fucking store closed. Instead of beans and a pack of Bull Durham I had to waste money on a pack of ready-mades out of a machine! Now I got fifty-three cents left and no beans! *Jesus*, I got to stop drinkin'!"

"What happened to eighty-five? I heard they was going to make him up again . . . What's that, he's already left?"

"Yeah," I said. "He's left. But I wasn't sorry to see that boxcar go. I must have been riding a badorder, the way it was shakin' and sway-ing."

"Naw, that was the tracks. I've been through there so goddamn many times amd it's always the same, they just don't keep up those old N.P. tracks."

He looked at me like he'd noticed me for the first time. "So you're going to Wenatchee to pick apples. What the hell you doing down here? Well, the apples'll wait. And there's plenty of apples—I ought to know, I thinned 'em. Too many apples, as a matter of fact. It was a dry year. Any time you got a mild winter and a dry year the apples get big. The trees are just covered. But I've never done any pickin'. Done thinnin', prunin', every other job in an orchard. But I guess a fella can learn. I'm going to stay out there—goin' to winter for a change where you don't have to fight the weather so. I was in Minneapolis last winter and I ain't going back for a while. You can freeze to death in that damn place, especially the way I was doing it. I was working outside, cleaning grain spills in the freight yard. I was working there until last week, yeah, as a matter of fact I worked eighty-nine and a half hours the last week I worked."

"That so," said the black man.

"That's what I said. Eighty-nine and a half hours. And I got a check stub to prove it." The tramp pulled a check stub from his overstuffed wallet and stuck it in our faces.

The black man said: "I used to know a fella down in El Paso used to pick that grain. Made good money."

"That guy is a millionaire, the guy *I* work for. He's down in Omaha now, cleaning up after a wreck. I could've went, but I started drinkin' . . ."

He changed the subject. "Usually I can tell where the cars are going. Now that lumber's goin' east, obviously. U.P., S.P. cars all going west. Santa Fe, too. Pretty soon all the reefers in the country will be goin' to Wenatchee and Walla Walla—you'll be able to pick apples pretty near 'til Christmas . . . Yeah, I know I can thin and I ought to be able to pick. Some of those guys make forty, fifty bucks a day. Payin' five, six bucks a bin, same as always . . ."

He told us he'd been drinking for ten days and it had cost him three hundred dollars he'd had in cash and seventy dollars he'd borrowed from a liquor store owner where he was a regular customer. He'd been drinking until the day he hit the road but he'd made the decision to get out of town before he was broke. He spent his last ten dollars on a quart of Canadian whiskey; the change, a dollar and three cents, he kept for food for the thousand-mile trip. When I saw him in Minneapolis he was anxious for the train to be underway so he could drink his last quart in peace. So a day later the binge ended in a hangover a thousand miles away on the wrong tracks in the middle of Montana.

Havre, Montana

eastbound along the Kootenai River, western Montana

looking for work in the "golden triangle"

Kalispell, Montana; Strawberry

Minot, North Dakota

bindle stiff; Havre, Montana

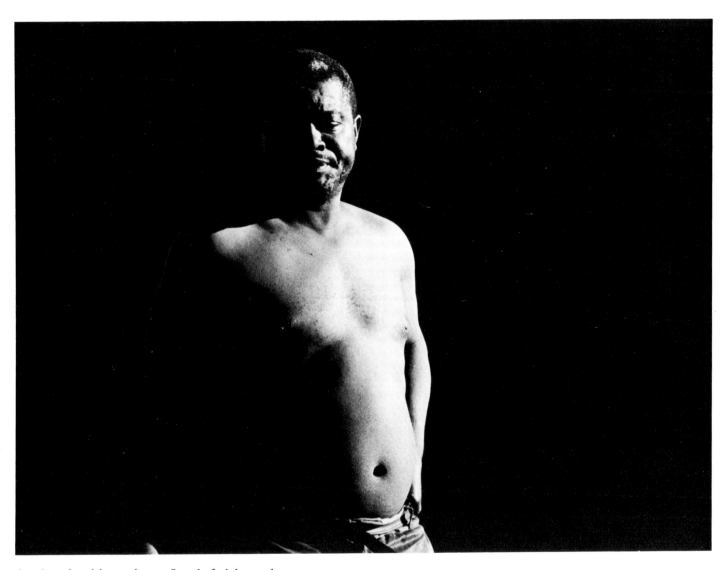

drunk and waiting to leave; Seattle freight yards

Havre, Montana

near Cutbank, Montana; autocarrier

waiting for an ambulance for a tramp who had been dragged under
a freight; yardmaster tries to cover lens

self-portrait

Seattle freight yard

Pend Oreille Lake, northern Idaho

Hippy Red and Queen of the Rails

northern Montana on the old Great Northern tracks

eastern Washington; apple knockers

The tramp gave himself hell for forgetting his food, ruining his clothes and wasting fifty cents on store bought cigarettes while missing the hotshot to Spokane, but he laughed at the drunk, the money spent, and the lost job. "Time to move," he said. "They were beginning to take advantage of me. And winter's comin' sooner than you think back there in Minni." Ripening apples two thousand miles away put him on the road, and the same scene would funnel thousands more into the northwest corner of the country. The workers would come and the crop would be harvested—then they'd drink up their money and be back on the road.

The train was finally made and the yard became quiet. The yard men went home to Sunday dinner and we headed out to find our cars.

I wondered how we'd split up for the trip. I expected the black man to go off by himself and he did, leaving me to travel with a beat-out old tramp, still coming down from his whiskey.

"You know," he said, as we were sitting waiting to go, "you can't trust everybody you meet. I can see it in your manner. You're too open, you're—what's the word—too naive."

"That may be, but you left your gear with me in the boxcar just now. I could've taken off with it."

"You weren't goin' nowhere. Got too much shit of your own. Anyway, you don't know enough to be afraid of. This life ain't no bed of roses you know. I've lost too much gear not to know that. You know how much this sleeping bag cost me? That's forty-five dollars right there. It's what they call a Red Fox. It's got that new-fangled material in it."

"It's good to travel with a sleeping bag," I said.

"Yeah, *if* you can keep it. You know the people you work with, they're bigger thieves than anybody. And then there are guys just to rob you, to git your money and your gear."

"Are these regular tramps you're talking about?"

"Well, they travel the country like your regular tramps, but they ain't no tramps. We call them jackrollers. And once in a while you'll get young kids that'll do the same thing. You just can't trust anybody, and I ain't kidding. Where we're headed, up there north of Wenatchee, that's country you got to be careful of. Ain't too bad goin' in, but comin' out, after the harvest, then you got to be careful. What I always do is make my wages and ride out of there payin'. Let that freight go all alone. And I seldom drink on the freight—I'll take it somewhere else.

"You got to understand something—you're just a tramp, and nobody wants nothun' to do with you unless it's your money or your work. The cops are no different. I got busted for drunk in Spokane last year, hell, I hadn't seen a bottle for three days! An' you always leave jail with clean pockets. But the worst ones are the jackrollers. See this one?" The tramp pointed to a scar that led from the corner of his left eye, down along his nose and across his lips. "That happened in Minneapolis. All they got off me that time was four dollars in cash and ten dollars' worth groceries."

"Were you drunk?"

"Hell, no, I was asleep. Woke up in the Hennepin County Hospital; they hit me in the face. Just missed my eye."

"Where were you stayin'?"

"I was *heading* west."

"Were you in a freight yard? In a boxcar?"

"Hell, no, I was out in the weeds. It's easy to find a man in a boxcar. You're a sitting duck in a boxcar. But they follow you out to the weeds, too. They watch, they watch for you and follow you out. *You'll* get it if you're not careful. I won't lay down in that boxcar, either, unless it's moving. And when that train is moving I got one eye open and I'm on my feet the moment he stops . . .

"You see, it's all changing. Used to be all you'd find on this road was the tramp, and this time of year the fruit tramp, what we call the apple knocker. But nowadays they're not all tramps. Seattle is so damn screwed up they'll come out of there to find work. And they're starting to get Mexicans in some places. Your real tramps won't associate with them. But most of the Mexicans stay down south, thinnin' beets, that's good work for them. Stoop labor, that's what they like. And the government's gettin' on a lot of camps where you'd live, closing them up. They're filthy places. But then there is no place for a man to stay. You have to carry a tent. I know some guys that do it,

14

carry a tent. Lightweight tents. And sometimes you'll build a shack. One guy will work days, the other nights. That way there'll always be somebody around to watch the stuff. But you got to be careful, really careful . . . I camped with a man and a woman last year and they stole what I had. Panasonic radio, worth forty dollars. AM/FM radio. Twelve bucks worth of groceries. And my bag with my change of clothes in it. But I know who they are and sooner or later I'll get them. You can't escape on this road—everybody knows you after a while . . .

"But you know, that's what gripes me. *I* ought to know my way around this road by now—I ought to be able to find my way out of Minneapolis! But I didn't think that was the right train last night. They run that hotshot late at night. Leaves the Burlington yards down in Chicago about the time we left Minneapolis."

"I knew it wasn't the hotshot," I interrupted, "but the braky told me it was a through freight to Minot. Figured I'd get to Minot, rest up and take a bath in that cattle watering tank by that jungle, and catch the hotshot in the morning."

"You could tell as soon as we got to Castleton that wasn't the Minot train. We jagged west in Castleton on the N.P. tracks. The 'Big G' went on north. Anyway you can't trust a brakeman. They usually just tell a man anything to get him out of the yards. You should have known they wouldn't be sending a freight up to Minot with all those flat cars! Those were headed for lumber country!"

"I suppose I should have known . . . I guess I wanted out of Minneapolis bad enough not to notice."

"Yeah, I'm the same way. I was on that train too."

"I was out in that lumber country last year about this time," I said, a bit later. "Jumped a train in Troy, Montana. I figured the train was changing crews so I was going up to the station to get some water."

"An' he took off."

"Right. That train left me standing there with six cents and no gear. Lucky I had a buddy in that car—threw out all the gear, then decided to jump himself! Skinned himself up good. It must have been a hundred degrees. We took a good swim in that river. What river is that, the Kootenai?"

"Yeah, and there's good trout there. Up Callahan Creek especially. You know where that bridge is down below there?"

15

"I remember it . . . But my buddy and I got the word that there hadn't been a freight stopped there for more than five years, and that the one we were on was just checking an overheating engine."

"You got to catch that local."

"There ain't no local no more. We hitched over to Libby, hung around there a long time trying to get a ride, and then we spent our last money on a passenger train to the division head in Whitefish where we picked up that hotshot again. We jumped out of that passenger train and there was that hotshot, all hooked and ready to go. The rest of the passengers headed up to that terminal, we ran over and grabbed the hotshot, and rode him all the way to Minot."

"Something else you gotta watch on this run," the tramp added, "They got a new bridge in Spokane. Out of the yards they can turn either left or right. And it's too late if you're on the wrong train, you haven't got a chance unless he stops up at Scropner, or Marshal. About fifteen or twenty miles out, and then you got to walk back. But goin' up that hill, just after the turn that will take you south to Pasco, sometimes he'll stop to set off some cars. You jump him there and then you've got to catch something coming back into town. Or walk."

"That makes a long trip to Wenatchee, through Pasco."

"There's certain times I don't care. In fact, there's a bean warehouse in Pasco where you can get all the beans you can carry. Damaged, but fine to eat . . . I don't care now, because I'll work hard enough once I get to Oroville to make up where I left off. This spring they were *begging* men to come up there. They couldn't get enough— nobody would work. Thinnin' and prunin' both, all work that's got to be done on schedule. Yeah, I made goddamn good money there this spring—a hundred sixty-eight bucks, in a little over two weeks. That'd be good money—*if* you could keep it. The truth of it's right here." He pointed to his hand. "Third wristwatch I've had this year."

"What about the wheat harvest? Can you get a job on a combine in this country?"

"You got to go up north, up to Havre, Shelby, around there. It's what they call the 'Golden Triangle'—Havre, Shelby, and Great Falls on the south. But if you want that kind of work I'd go to Walla Walla. Pays better money. They're payin' twenty dollars a day in Washington. Montana never goes past a buck seventy-five an hour . . .

"I've done all that work. Chopped cotton in Fresno, California. Drove a labor bus, worked on ranches all over Montana. Worked for a labor contractor named Speedy in California, but they run him out of the state. I guess he's somewhere in Oregon now.

He changed the subject. "When I walked up town just now I walked by a bunch of those little crabapple trees but they were in somebody's yard—I just couldn't get in there. And a whole bunch of those small red plums. Just loaded, them trees. I'd like to have a sack of those! Most of this country is *rainin'* fruit! Peaches, pears, apples, cherries . . . I ate so many of those cherries in Wenatchee—man, I got the shits! It was that orchard right by the yards. Just a small grove of trees. I didn't have any food and I wasn't sure I could get any of those foodstamps."

Foodstamps! The word had an odd ring. I glanced at the tramp; his eyes were downcast. In the tramp world how one gets by when you're down on your luck becomes a matter of great importance. The mission stiff, no longer able to make it on the outside, is least respected. Yet I'd traveled with men who called themselves "foodstamp tramps," and moved, as had tramps always, from one free hit of food to another. Perhaps the foodstamp tramp was merely the most modern of a long tradition of tricksters—but at the same time it didn't smell right. The tramp didn't belong in a government office filling out forms. It did not seem an honorable form of begging; the encounter in which the tramp proves himself—the manipulation of the sympathy of another—was absent.

But when you're down on your luck you get a little help from others on the road. The sharing is complex even though it is simple. You can take for a time, but you must give in return, somewhere down the line. I offered the tramp one of my last sandwiches and he at first refused it because, I think, it was beneath his dignity to accept food from someone he regarded as a rather inept novice. But after a time his hunger overcame his pride and he took a squashed peanut butter sandwich over to the corner to eat by himself. He did, however, ask me what the fuck I was doing with *peanut butter sandwiches*—where, boy, were the beans?

The train finally left Laurel and crawled slowly toward Helena. We rode in an oversized boxcar, and standing before the twelve-by-twenty-foot door was like standing on a chair in the second row of a wide-screen movie. But the ride was slow and gentle for a while, and half of the sky was laced in the purple and pink of a prairie sunset. The tramp stood by me and pointed out camps and jungles where he'd stayed at one time or another during the past twenty-five years, and places where he said the trout were so thick they'd jump right out of the water into your frying pan. The signs of hobo habitation would have gone unnoticed—a bit of refuse around an old fire, usually under a bridge, or even just some matted grass and some old cans in a pile. Back behind a bridge was a shack made from tarpaper and crates; and as we passed, an old 'bo stuck his head out and waved. The tramp said he'd stayed in that very same shack, with different *tarpaper,* but still the same *shack,* seven years before while he waited for a job on a ranch.

The tramp softened up as he told me stories over the noise of the slow-moving train. I mostly kept quiet, trying to decide if I was glad to be in the company of a man I had little reason to trust. When darkness fell I became too tired to consider the matter further, and I fell asleep hoping to wake with my gear by my side.

Sometime in the night I woke again; the train had stopped. When my eyes adjusted to the dark I saw the tramp, perched by the door keeping watch. He told me we were in Helena and that he'd already left to find out if our train was staying together and moving further west. He'd left his gear with me and said that he'd hoped that anyone trying to steal it would have made enough noise to wake me up. I tried to stay awake but kept falling asleep. After short periods I would wake, startled by dreams, and always to find the tramp by the door, keeping watch.

By sunrise, four through-freights had passed our train. We were still made up but stranded on a siding off the main track. We were, it seemed, waiting for more engines for the trip over the Rockies. Finally, when the sun was still low in the sky, the power we had been waiting for idled into position. There were two engines, magnificently powerful even with their strength bound up in slow rhythmic throbbing. The engines were jockeyed into the middle of the train and we were off once more.

For an entire morning the train pulled up the Rockies. Even with the six engines wide open the freight often slowed to ten or fifteen miles an hour. The smell of pines filled the car and the mountains stretched out below. I stayed by the door and watched while the tramp sat, lost in his own world. Near noon we pulled onto a siding on the top of the mountain, left the extra power behind and raced down into Missoula, where we were switched off the main line and onto a siding. Our bull local was at the end of the line.

"I didn't see anything made up heading west," the tramp said, "so it'll be three or four hours before we get out of here. Christ, I wish I'd caught that hotshot yesterday! . . . I'd be in Spokane, maybe Wenatchee by now! . . . But did you see those apple trees coming into the yard? They were loaded. I think I might take a walk over there and see if I can't get us some fresh fruit!"

I had a couple of dollars and some change. The apple trees were near a small store, so I gave the tramp some of the change to restock our supplies. As the store was about a mile away I settled in for more waiting.

I was dozing when the train jerked ahead, then slammed backward. I was sitting with the tramp's gear and the train was pulling out. I was going to jump but figured that the tramp might catch the tail end to meet up with me at the next division. But if I stayed with the train and left the tramp behind I'd be one more thief ripping off his gear. The brakelines were hooked up fast and the train started rolling forward. There was only one thing to do—I threw the tramp's gear, then mine, and jumped as the train was picking up speed. I was about a mile down the line, so I headed back. There was another freight ready to go on the main line north.

It was hot and I was tired. I couldn't carry all the gear in one load, so I had to move a load ahead and return for the rest. I came across a brakeman who seemed to enjoy the sight of me dragging gear all over his yard.

"Have you seen an old man up that way? He's got a week's beard, dirty, smelly bastard . . ."

"Sure, yeah, I've seen plenty of them," he answered, "what's the big deal?"

I ignored him and went off, finally stopping on a small rise near the westbound freight. The train was ready to go—brakelines hitched and

19

crummy moving into position. I was about to leave the tramp's gear in a pile and move into the first empty, but he showed up with a sack full of apples and groceries before I made the move.

"Where have *you been*?" I yelled.

"You got my gear?"

"Yeah, I got your gear . . . What you carryin', rocks?"

He snorted at me and headed for the train. We moved into the first empty, a beat-up old car with metal walls that radiated the afternoon sun like an oven. It wasn't much of a car, but at that point in our jackrabbit trip across Montana we'd have been happy with the rustiest badorder on the Burlington Northern tracks. As it turned out, that's about what we got.

The tramp told me I'd given him sixty-one cents which, with the last of his money, had come to a dollar four. He'd bought two cans of beans, a loaf of day-old bread, and a ten-cent pack of Bull Durham rolling tobacco, which came with papers. The groceries had cost a dollar and four cents.

We were halfway through our meal when I asked the tramp: "How'd you get started in all this?"

"Army. I started running around in the army. I been *all* over . . ."

"Where did you come from before the army?"

"Wisconsin," the tramp said between mouthfuls, "Janesville, Wisconsin. I was in the Army six and a half years—fought in the second world war. Reenlisted in 1946. Pretty near '47. Born in 1923—I'm no *kid*, you know . . ."

"Did you ever settle down? Most people run around a few years, then settle down."

"Not me . . . I worked too many years, off and on you know, for different people—six months here, eight months there. I git tired of what I'm doin' and just move on, go on to the next one . . .

"See, I don't *have* to work at all. I can make it fine without working. But let's see—I've done all kinds of work. I drove a lot of tractors in this country, seeding—that kind of thing. That farm work is easy, but I get bored. Find myself looking for something else."

"I've done some migrating around," I said, "working at different kinds of things. But I keep thinking there will be an end point—I've got the idea that I'll go back to one place although I can't seem to figure out what place that will be. I guess you have to be married to settle down like that . . ."

"I suppose so," the tramp answered, "I never got married and I never settled down, so I guess I can't say."

"Are there places you like more than others? Places you keep going back to?"

"Nope."

"But some places are easier to live in than others."

"Oh, yeah, that's different. There's better living where it's warmer. But usually when you get something good like that, something else balances it out. Maybe the people you got to live with, work with, ain't no good. Most things balance out; it comes out pretty even in the end . . .

"Back to Bull Durham cigarettes!" the tramp laughed. "Quite a comedown, I been smokin' tailor-mades for a month now. Yeah, I know plenty of guys—that's all they live on—beans and Bull Durham. These guys know where they can get all their food for nothin', that's *if* they're in the mood to go get it. Like there's a bean warehouse in Tally, shit, if you carry a hundred pounds you can take it! Then you can go bum the butcher, and get some meat. All you need is salt. In Pasco you can get all the potatoes you can carry—onions, too. They're layin' on the ground behind the warehouses. It ain't perfect-*lookin'* food all the time, but it's fine to *eat* . . .

"You need rope?" the man asked me, suddenly.

I didn't need the rope, but I didn't want to insult the tramp by refusing his offer. I told him: "I don't need it now, but I might later. Why don't you carry it."

"You sure? Christ, I got plenty. I didn't think to look at the length of it and when I finally looked I discovered it was a goddamn clothesline!"

A train rolled by. "That's the old Milwaukee Road! An electric train, like those we passed. Can you hear the difference—the way it sounds? They're really just like diesels—they just get their electricity from that big wide contraption on top of the train that pushes up on that cable—the diesel burns its fuel to get electricity. You don't see many electrics—and that old Milwaukee Road is about finished up. I used to work for the Milwaukee Road; I was a 'white hat,' assistant foreman, for a while after I got discharged. I got that job through a friend, not through knowledge. All we was doin' was raisin' the rails. You know when a car sways, like the other night on the N.P.—that's because the joint supports are low. Then when one is low the next one on the opposite side gets pushed down, too. The car will hit one and go this way; they hit the other and go that way. So you get down on your knees and crawl down that railroad. You sight down along and have somebody mark it—then they jack it up till you tell them to stop. Up and down until it's right.

"I did that for a long time. If I'd stayed I could have retired by now. Hell, if I'd stayed I'd have my pension by now!

"But I've been a jack-of-all-trades. Truck drivin', farmin', a little carpentry work. You got to work like that on this road. You got to take any job and do it and you can't be fussy. If the people say they want you to rake the lawn you go rake the lawn. Or if they want you to shovel shit out of the chicken coop you go an' do that. You can't be fussy—and you can't be fussy about your wages. If you get fussy you get a bad name, and you get known for it! You get known by those on the road, and those alongside the road. They'll know you are with me—I'll bet some of them know already! Up in that Wenatchee country there's a lot I know. Woody's up there and that guy who owes me the twenty—he's up there. Boo-Hoo Red's up there—they'll all be pickin'. Red'll be up with Doc English—they wanted me to come back, that's where I trimmed this spring. But it's a bad place to live—the cabins are terrible." He shrugged his shoulders. "Hell, it's like anything else, it's what you make it. You get yourself a bad name—nobody'll have you."

"I didn't figure you were known much," I said, "I thought you'd come in, another face, another body to work—you know, what the hell!"

"No, you're wrong. They've known me for years. Christ, I'm a *real* oldtimer now. I worked sheepherding in this country too. And this is the longest you'll see me out of work—about a week, maybe ten days at the most—and sometimes not even that. I work hard, and I'll get a regular bankroll. Last year when I took a bus into Spokane I had over fifteen hundred in my pocket! Sure, I looked a little different—had a haircut, clean clothes—but that's the way it is, up and down . . ."

We sat for some minutes without talking. The engines were attached, brakelines hooked together; everything was set, but the freight didn't move. Finally, to break the silence, I said: "By the way, my name's Doug."

The tramp looked up, startled. Then he answered: "Carl." It was an awkward exchange; I wished I'd had a handle so I could have said: "Back where I come from they call me Highball Harper." This way it was too personal—I felt like I was moving too close, crowding a loner. But the distance was maintained by the tramp; he never called me by my name.

He pulled out his wallet and began sorting the papers. Check stubs came out, one after another, all weeks of long hours at minimum wages. I sensed the tramp was establishing to me his identity as a working man but he laughed and said: "All I really carry that is important is my social security card and this," he extended a frayed card to me, "my Timex watch guarantee."

"You've got to be kidding! You said you had three of them taken off you this year!"

"Yeah, and I got a new guarantee each time. And this stuff," he pulled out a wad of coupons, "this stuff is just like money. Here's a coffee coupon—twenty cents on Maxim's—here's twenty cents for Folgers. Here's a receipt for rent where I lived for a while last winter—the old Palace Hotel on 216 University Southwest. It was near where I was workin' but they were tearin' it down and the housing authority paid me two hundred twenty-five dollars to move out! Easiest money I remember in a long time . . ."

The buzzing of a fly reverberated through the car; otherwise the afternoon was still and lifeless. We seemed to have run aground once more. One short division across a third of the length of Montana in twenty-four hours! I became angry at the frustration of our trip and took a walk to stretch my muscles and cool my mind, and to leave the unnervingly stoic presence of the tramp. Things were settled for him; his hangover had worn away, his stomach was full of beans and he had enough tobacco for the thousand-mile trip that lay ahead. It was up to me to still my impatience and learn again the pace of tramp traveling.

23

The tramp seemed to sense my mood. "You know," he said as I climbed back into the car, "you're heading out to good country. You can have a steady job in that country—make good money. This spring I was makin' two dollars an hour and all I was doin' was thinnin'. After a year I went back and he says, 'Carl, *I* don't need anybody, but a neighbor of mine does—you can work for *him*.' 'All right,' I says . . . I didn't tell him I never done any thinnin'. But I learned fast. In a little over two weeks—I was getting two dollars a tree there—I made five hundred sixty-five dollars. When I work I work hard! Few people can keep up with me—I get soakin' wet just workin'. One day—that was up at 'Haskell, Burns and Kernin'—the boss came by and made me stop! He said, 'You sit down and take a break!' That's how hard I was workin', digging out irrigation pipes this spring. *That's* a job, and he wanted me to stay around."

"But you wouldn't have it, though, huh?"

His voice lowered. "I started drinkin' . . . Had a couple of Arkies I had to live with, I couldn't stomach that!"

"Do you figure drinking gets in the way of things you want to do sometimes?"

"Not if I don't want it to!" he said sharply. "You're thinking of those on skid row, and we're not the same at all. They just don't want to do nuthin'! They just sit there and bum—you can't get one of them to work if you tried! They even bum from each other; steal from each other, too. I'll go out and work for a man . . .

"You see, he explained, "the oldtimer's gone. The *good* tramp, the *real* tramp, he's dead. Now it's the young fellow taking over. They rob, steal—the oldtimer made about a division a day, if he wanted to. Sometimes not even that. He'd stay there a week—maybe ten days—and he'd make his own camp and it'd be clean. There'd be a mirror in the tree hanging up, maybe a frying pan all clean, pots and pans all clean, and wood for the fire. And you left it the same way. Guys don't do that no more today. Punch a hole in the pan, or take it along. Or throw it away.

"Things been changing in the past fifteen, maybe twenty years. Now most of them get their foodstamps and they eat right out of the can. Don't even cook up proper any more. I know where all of them are, on this route especially."

"How did the oldtimers get their money together?"

24

"They worked, periodically. They got a different philosophy of life, you know, those old 'boes. They were really a throwback, something like a mountain man. They can go out with nothin' and make a living. Just the clothes on their back. Most people can't do that. They'd freeze to death, or starve. But some of us go three, four, or even five days without eating. And think nothin' about it. That's because we're good and tough. But I get into that alcohol, that's my trouble . . ." His voice became softer, "Hell, I used to teach school, in the army."

"Really, no kidding . . ."

"Sure, I was a small arms instructor. Aberdeen proving grounds, if you ever heard of that."

"No, I can't say I have."

"Small arms; weapons. And I used to be a supply sergeant in the army."

After a pause I asked: "Tell me more about those old guys . . ."

"Oh, there's a few of them left—you hear about them by name. But I have a hard time remembering them. Let's see, there's Jake the Fake—he got his pension, yeah, he's livin' in Spokane. He retired, but he's still known. He'd go through your pack sack if he were here. You watch, if you stick around me very much, we'll see some of the guys. They'll ask me about the man and woman who stole my good radio and good clothes—that was old Delores and Dusty. Then there's Big Red, Texas Louie, all them kind of guys. The Denver Kid—that kind of bullshit. You got a million Blackies—some people call *me* Blackie. I got a big black beard, although it's getting white now—and I'm dark complected."

"So you've been on this road a long time . . ."

"Not this road. I usually travel west on the Great Northern, or the Milwaukee. You see, this is called the 'Nigger Pacific.' N.P.—Nigger Pacific. The niggers built it and they ride it. They came up on the high line and got their ass kicked. The Milwaukee Road—they wouldn't ride it because it was too slow for them."

"Are there as many people riding the freights as there used to be," I interrupted, "or is it dying out?"

"There's more. But not the tramp, like I was saying. A lot of them are young guys, like you. That's why I'm careful. Because they're the ones who take you—they took me twice this year already. I already told you, the life is dyin' out because the oldtimer is just about gone.

25

But there is people ridin'. Some of them are thieves, and most of them only make trouble of one sort or another. Hell, I went to sleep in Newport a couple of months ago and when I woke up my gear was gone! Even my wristwatch was gone! I'd like to know how they got that off me without waking me . . . They even took my ropes—I had good nylon ropes, about the size of my little finger that I used, you know, for tyin' things up."

"But you left your things with me. Weren't you afraid I'd do like the rest?"

He snorted. "You weren't goin' nowhere—I can judge a guy right away and you were nothing to worry about. You watch—you're going to get burned. They'll talk good—an' you'll believe them, real nice guys in front of your face—then watch! You got to be careful when you go to work up there! Don't carry too much money with you. Have the boss keep your money until you're ready to leave and then have him take you right to the depot. Bank to the depot. For Chrissake, don't ride a freight out of there. Bank to depot, out you go!"

"A lot of this is new to me," I said, "I got a lot to learn."

"It ain't like Minneapolis, you know. Hell, in Minneapolis I walk around with five, six hundred dollars in my pocket and think nothin' of it. But I don't flash it. I keep that roll in one pocket and my change in another. Money is dangerous now because it's so short. But even when I was makin' big money I had to spend it, you can't save nothing! I went to the grocery store one day in Oroville—you know how much my bill was? Sixty-six dollars—just meat, coffee, butter, normal things a man has got to eat when he is workin'. Yep, first week was forty-five, the second was sixty-five. Of course the guy I was stayin' with—he'd take a roast—fry it up like a steak and eat it in one meal! That's old Crooked-Stem Smitty. He's out there, he's there somewhere. I never saw a man eat so much in all my life. I'd take a big pot, stew, or beans, or maybe spaghetti—maybe elbow macaroni mixed with hamburger and tomato sauce, you know what I mean—I'd eat what I wanted and I'll be damned if he wouldn't sit there and eat the rest!

"Come on train, it's twenty-five to two!" Carl finally began to show his restlessness. "It'll be the middle of the night before we hit Spokane! Yeah, I made this trip once before like this—the same god-

26

damn train—this old workin' bull local, back and forth between the divisions . . ."

"I figured on the same time it took last time—thirty-five hours."

"You can do it that way on the high line. *If* you can stand the ride. That's up on what we still call the Great Northern—although it's all Burlington Northern now. Up there, hell, there's three time the trains, and they're hot ones. If we'd caught out of Minneapolis the way we should have we'd be sittin' up north of Wenatchee now, lookin' for work!"

He looked disgusted with himself. "Hell, I got to wash my clothes! If I could get alongside a river I'd get clean. I've got a shirt, pants, gloves in my pack—and that's just a few of the clothes I got. Christ, they're scattered all over, and I'm going to have to get my hands on some winter gear pretty soon—I'm going to winter out here this time around. It's not so cold and if I stay in an orchard it don't cost me much to live. The food is higher but it ain't that much different and in the orchards I can cook it myself. You don't have to go five or six miles to work—your cabin's right down there in the orchard. But when you get a job where you got to waste time—that's what hurts! Remember those check stubs I showed you? Well, I wouldn't work for that Hutchinson no more! Those damn trees, you can't reach them with a fourteen-foot ladder! they've never been pruned and you can't set a ladder in them, even to thin 'em. You get half the apples pickin' trees like that for the same work . . ."

The tramp peered at me and changed the subject: "I saw you lookin' for me, dragging my gear all over."

"I was going to sit in that boxcar for a while but when it started moving out of the yards I jumped him . . ."

"I saw you waitin' on that high piece of ground and I knew you weren't goin' nowhere so I stayed where I was and took my time pickin' these apples."

"You almost saw the last of me," I said, "I rode the train back and forth three times and when it started pulling out of the yard I almost stayed on it. Thought you might have caught him on the tail end."

"So you almost rode him out of here, eh?" The tramp cocked an eye at me. "Yeah, for a while I wondered where you were . . . I saw the train shifting around there . . ."

27

" 'I wondered where you were'! I figured you were sitting in that bar having a cold one with our money! . . . Boy, that'd taste good now—a nice cold beer!"

The tramp said: "I'd just as soon have lemonade!" He paused, then added: "I'm over it now for a while—and anyway I don't drink beer, I drink whiskey. Canadian whiskey. Oh, when I start, maybe I'll have two or three beers, but that's all—then it's my Canadian booze . . .

"Yeah, when I drink like that I don't know what the hell I'm doing . . ."

We fell into a silence that matched the heaviness of the afternoon. At last, as shadows were getting longer, the train found its power and we headed toward another hump of the Rockies and the city of Spokane.

The afternoon's travel was broken by a two-hour wait on a siding only an hour north of Missoula. Finally an Amtrak passenger train sped past and we reclaimed our tracks to begin another ascent of the Rockies. The late afternoon sun kept slipping behind the mountains, then reappearing as we climbed higher and higher. The train worked hard and the ride was slow. Hours were spent without conversation, and in the privacy of our trip I felt a deep loneliness. As we passed one of the few towns on the route—Thompson Falls, Montana—the train veered close to the houses and I watched people through their windows, sitting down to supper. The tramp crouched in his corner, by now just a dark shadow. I felt lost in the din of the train and the approaching darkness.

It was completely dark by the time we reached the top. The extra engines were left on a siding and then we careened down the other side of the mountain. The freight moved faster than any I have ridden and our boxcar threw us around like the wood chips that covered the floor. For hours we sped directly northwest; then the train turned west and the ride became tamer as we crossed the flatlands of Idaho. City lights appeared in the distance, and we entered Spokane. I felt done in by the ride and the long day but the tramp seemed newly energized. We jumped the train as it idled into the yards and hiked to a huge bridge where there was a freight in the making. I guessed that it was after midnight.

The tramp wandered off, again leaving me with all our gear, to determine the destination of the train. I felt immobilized and vulnerable. I tried to shrink into the shadows, but passing figures, if they noticed me at all, paid me no heed. A yard engine idled by, illuminating me in its glare and startling me with its bell. Boxcars loomed as black shapes as they creaked through the yard.

Carl finally returned, satisfied that he'd found the Wenatchee train. I was anxious to find a place to ride but we were out of water and Carl wouldn't think of traveling dry. He again disappeared into the darkness to return a few minutes later with two gallon bottles full to the brim with ice water.

"Where in the hell did you get those?" I asked.

"Shhh," he whispered, "not so loud." He started pouring the water into our canteen and hilex bottle. "See that tail end dragging the crummy around the yard? I knew nobody would be riding that crummy while they was pushing it through the yard so I jumped in and borrowed this here water. I knew it would be in the refrigerator. Always is."

"You mean you went right into a caboose to get this water? Isn't the door locked?"

"Naw, the door's never locked."

"But the light's on inside of those things. It's like daylight!"

"You can do a lot of things in the light of day," he answered, "providing you move real quick! Now hold steady so I can pour!"

We left the bottles in full view ("We don't need the bottles—just the water," the tramp said) and began walking down the train, each to a side. We learned quickly to adjust our pace so we would meet at each coupling. We found an empty boxcar near the end of the train and boarded.

Carl spoke in whispers: "I been through this yard for years but I know the other yard, the old Great Northern, better. Back where they used to run the high line. That's the old N.P. It's only lately—since they merged—that the Big G comes through here . . . That's a good yard over there. Store nearby. Water easy to get. Then there's the

"Yardley Tavern" a half a block down the street. An old woman run it."

"I guess these yards aren't so complicated," I said, "but sometimes I walk into one of them and I don't know where in the hell to start. I waste time, and I miss trains that way . . ."

"But you don't even know what to watch for!" the tramp interrupted. "Half the time you don't even know where the mainlines are! You got to learn while you're hanging around! For instance, in this yard they make up all the trains right here. The rest of the yard don't mean a thing to you. The hotshot stays on the main line. They just check him on the main line—maybe reshuffle his cars over the hump—and send him right back out."

"But even the hotshots bust up here, don't they?"

"Not here! They go right on through. They're made up way east—Minneapolis, Chicago. That Seattle train's made up right in St. Paul. It don't bust up in Minot—they just shuffle the train over the hump and the same cars go out again. It's ninety-seven and one-ninety-seven—that's their numbers. Odd numbers going west; even going back east."

"Do those numbers mean the train leaves the same time, travels the same route? Or is it something else?"

"It's the same train. It's the 'time freight.' That's another name for it. We were on a drag—that's the local we've been stuck on for the last couple of days."

"Last year they told me I was riding a hotshot and it busted up all over the place," I said.

"Well, they said it was the hotshot. The only real hotshots are ninety-seven and one-ninety-seven. The *through* freight; the *time* freight. They got to keep time. The others, they just fuck around, go onto 'hold' and let the hot ones go through . . .

"There's a lot of tricks to it. It's always better not to have to ask anybody nuthin'. After you done it a few times you can recognize the engines and tell where the train is going. Look at that engine over there—that's a 'square nose.' Out of Laurel they go to Salt Lake. If it's a 'round nose,' they'll go up the high line. It's what we had on tonight. The round nose'll have a headlight right out in front. A single light. The new Burlington Northerns—they're sort of pointed but we call them square nosed because the angles are sharp in front of the engines . . .

"Now usually the S.P. & S. comes up here. They'll put the S.P. & S. and the Great Northerns together. But when they go down to Salt Lake they put a Western Pacific on it. So there you are—the next time you ought to be able to get out of Laurel!"

"Well, what about Salt Lake City—that a hot yard?"

"No, no, that's a good yard. A lot of guys go there. You'll find a lot headed for Ogden—that's outside Salt Lake—because they get a hundred and fifty-some dollars a month welfare. And out of Salt Lake you can go anywhere you want to. Denver, you catch the Burlington. Or, if you want to get to Denver you can go down through Billings. You got to know your connections. You can go through Wyoming from Laurel, or you can go through Nebraska. Or you can go north to Great Falls—all that from Laurel, right where we were."

"I liked that land between here and Laurel," I said, "I really liked it this time. I wanted to see it that way—to go through the mountains during the day—and I'm glad I did."

Carl surprised me by replying: "That north route's better; I like that ride through Glacier Park. You can see the whole canyon. You can see all the way up to the top, and then when you go down the other side, through west Glacier, you get another view of that whole goddamn valley. But then once you get past Cutbank you don't see much scenery any more, just wheatland all the way past Havre, Shelby, all the way to Minot. All of a sudden, bang! Corn country. Corn and those goddamn sunflowers."

"That eastern Montana on the high line is a barren damned area . . . Glasco, Wolf Point . . . doesn't seem to be much there."

"Had good crops there last couple of years. But before that, too much rain, not enough rain—nuthin would grow up there!"

I broke the lull: "That ride last night—I'm sore! Boy . . ."

"Tonight was worse!" Carl said. "That dirty cocksucker, rocking all the way. Why, my insides were goin' back and forth, bouncin' like that and then that damn slamming back and forth!" He looked at our bags along the walls in the front of the car and said: "It's dangerous layin' the way we are now. If we stop real quick, our heads are goin' right up through the wall. If he stops quick and you're layin' side-

31

ways, you roll—hell, I already lived through one wreck! That was in California. Feather River. He throwed about a dozen cars off and I didn't even wake up! Shit, I woke up in a siding the next day and we stayed there for three days—in a snowbank. It was just gettin' spring. Lucky I had a whole sack of french bread and rolls, some lunch meat, and even some old coffee. No tobacco though. Spring nearby so I could get water easy. But dammit, it was cold! Couldn't do much except sit!"

"I always stayed out of California when I've been on the freights. I sort of assumed that those yards would be hot."

"They're all right—again, that's if you know them. What I do sometimes is, if I'm in Oakland, which is hot, is to hitchhike, or if I got the money, take the bus up to Stockton, or even Oroville. The yard's smaller and it ain't hot. You can pick up a hotshot out of there that goes two ways. One goes to Salt Lake City and the other comes up here.

"You can get down there, all right. Catch out of Portland, which can be tricky, or better to go through Wishram. Pasco to Wishram and then the S.P. & S., or the Western Pacific to California. Wishram is the next division goin' down the river out of Pasco. Breaks up there in Wishram, puts it back together and away he goes! Up the mountain—up the Columbia River canyon—and shit, that's pretty. You follow that Deschutes River all the way to the top. Over a hundred miles. Then you go through Bend, Klamath Falls, Redding, and then down to Oroville. You can ride into Oakland, you just got to be careful. It's going out that's tough."

Our conversation was blotted out by an Amtrak passenger train highballing through the yard. It was a short train, not more than ten cars, with no intention of slowing for the Spokane freight yard. Our train suddenly snapped forward and threw us both off our feet. Carl lost his balance and nearly fell out of the car.

"Don't tell me, I ducked!" he said as the train began idling westward. "I remember the first time that happened. It scared the daylights out of me. About this time of the night and that train let go—I didn't know what was happening! The train snapped and I must have gone three feet into the air . . .

"When you hear something like that you duck. God, I've seen a man get his head cut off! He was stickin' it out and lookin'—door open about this much and it slammed shut—there it goes! That's it! Christ, what a bloody mess! Hands, same thing. I've seen 'em bust off their feet sittin' hanging them out the door and wham! Those switches or those close bridges I showed you. You can't see them coming. *Never* sit with your feet hangin' out the side of the car. *Never!* Even standing here like we are, if that thing jerks—out you go! It don't take much . . ."

We idled near a lighted caboose. "See that crummy over there," said the tramp, "that's where I got the water. Just go over and check if the door's open and if it is, go right in. If they find you rummaging around in there you say, 'Hey, where's this train goin' ' while you're making for the door! . . . Naw, there's nothing to worry about. If it's their own crummy, they'll lock it. Some crews ride the same train and keep the same crummy—but they don't do that much any more. Years ago they kept their own caboose a certain way. You didn't mess around with those." The train snapped to a stop. In the distance we heard an amplified voice directing the making of another midnight train. We were still deep in the yards.

The tramp bent over his small bag to roll a cigarette. The couplings creaked and groaned and the train nudged ahead.

"Nowadays everything's mechanized on these jobs so you can't stop and roll a smoke. You gotta buy tailor-mades. Or at least I wouldn't stop working to roll a smoke. I'd think the boss was lookin' at me."

The train picked up speed and the tempo and the intensity of the noise increased. Rock, rattle, bang bang bang. There were dim fires near the edge of the tracks where, Carl said, the Indians and the niggers jungle, and where I'd stay away from if I knew what I was doing.

"See, there's somebody over there!" Carl pointed ahead. The tramp saw us and yelled: "Which way's he goin'?" Carl hesitated before he answered and the tramp was past our car when he yelled: "Seattle."

"I didn't want anybody in this car," he said, "that's why I waited until we went by to answer. He sounded like a drunk Indian anyway."

"I noticed you didn't tell him this was the Wenatchee train, either."

"That tramp won't know if this is the Wenatchee train because it goes both ways to Seattle. I ended up in Pasco that way once. The train was goin' to Seattle but it went the long way around and I missed Wenatchee by a few hundred miles." We passed more jungle fires.

33

"That's where they coop up, under that bridge. You got to stay on the other side of that bridge, away from here. They get their water in those stock yards. That's Armour packing. Then they go up a little ways and get a free meal from St. Vincent de Paul's. They hang around down there, I *know*. That's why I don't like to bed down comin' out of these yards. Anybody can jump in—and if it's a Negro I won't let him in. Maybe if he's alone I'd let him in. If there's two of them, no way. Either they'd get out, or I would. I'd just tell them there's another car down back. There's more than one empty on a train—they can get their own car! It's bad at night, especially this time of year with all the pickers coming in . . . and if you been drinking, watch out!"

"I don't drink when I'm riding," I said.

"Well, if I do drink I get up the corner of the car. Even when I got a hangover, you won't see me near the door. Fuck no! I stay in the back but I get scared! The speed raises hell with me—I just don't like it anymore."

"I don't drink on the road, and I figure I can handle most that are drunk. Or at least that's what I tell myself. People get crazy when they drink. Sometimes they don't seem rational . . . They just do crazy things . . ."

But Carl answered: "Oh, you can handle a drunk if you know what you are doing. But if you drink yourself—then it's bad. Or if two or three of them that's been drinkin' jump you."

"Yeah, I've been told plenty of times never to let a couple of guys entice me into a car with a bottle . . ."

"No, no, *fuck* no! Don't ever ride with a couple of them. Your best bet is to get with an oldtimer, somebody that knows the ropes. Nine times out of ten that oldtimer will be carryin' a gun—especially in this country. I used to carry a gun, not no more. Afraid I'd kill somebody. Used to herd sheep in this country—you needed one there. And I carried one for a long time in the army—anyway it's all how you use it. People fuck around with them but I tell you, buddy, if you go pulling a gun you better use it! 'Cause if you don't, you won't be around to tell about it!"

Under another bridge Carl pointed to more jungles. "All along here—you watch during the day. Old fires all over. It's bad here, too, if you come down take the street, or walk along the highway and climb down by that first bridge . . . Yeah, there's a lot of tricks on this road, but only a few important ones. You have to learn to stay away from the rest. Set up camp after dark. I never let anybody know where I'm goin'—I wait until the campfire's out and then I disappear. I don't want nobody to follow me!" Then he looked me straight in the eye. "Some people on this road are helpless. When you start helpin' it's just like having a son—they don't know where it stops! You got to support them—take care of them—you got to provide the hand and I won't do that. If a fella is on this road and he can't learn—then to hell with him!"

"You get tired of me just let me know!"

"I will, but you still don't know what I mean. Don't travel alone if you can help it, but when you get your job, don't depend on nobody else. If you want to leave, then leave! That's it—a lot of these guys say, 'If you quit, let me know and I'll quit with you.' I say *bullshit*. Before you know it you'll have run out of places to work."

"That why you been leaving all these good jobs you've been telling me about?"

"Usually I get tired of the man. I work hard for a man but after a while he thinks he owns me! He starts puttin' more and more work on me with the same pay. I say to hell with that—that's when I leave. But I don't care how cold and rough it gets, you won't find me on the bum. It might be forty below but I'll find work. Maybe just for my clothes and some warmth, and a little food, but I'll work. And I ain't proud." We passed an intersection in the tracks. "I was right—there goes that Pasco cutoff!" Carl yelled. We crossed a valley on a bridge that seemed to go on forever. Carl said the valley was three hundred feet below but it was all lost in the darkness. The ride was smooth and fast when I bedded down and I was asleep in minutes.

6

We arrived in Wenatchee before dawn. We jumped the train as it stopped to change crews and hiked along the tracks into the main yards, then to a creek where Carl said we'd find a jungle. I was stumbling along more asleep than awake wishing I'd ridden that train down the road to a hot breakfast but Carl was full of energy. He found the camp, cleaned some of the junk away and stacked our gear in a pile. It was a dreary place, a pile of burned rocks, some bent-up five-gallon cans for seats, an old rusty grill, and a small stack of wood. There were tin cans and broken bottles scattered everywhere. The wood was green and Carl used up half a pack of matches trying to make a fire. I watched him without saying much and when he went down into the ravine to find better wood and some cans to heat water in I stayed behind. I sat there with my teeth chattering, waiting for a fire I didn't feel like making and wishing there'd be something for breakfast besides beans.

He came up with an armload of wood and went back down to fill our canteens. I'd begun to wonder where he'd gone when he came trudging up the hill with two five-pound coffee cans, both nearly new, and an old hilex bottle. He cut the hilex bottle off to use as a washbasin and promised to keep such prize coffee cans for at least the next thousand miles. I sat and watched as he built the fire.

A westbound freight idled through the yards. Ten or twelve tramps huddled together on a piggyback. "Probably too drunk to get off," Carl grunted, "ain't no reason to go to Seattle this time of year!"

As the fire began to burn well, Carl balanced the filthy, rusty grate between tall, slab-shaped rocks that formed the edge of the fire. He filled the cleanest can with water and placed it on the grate to heat.

"We're going to need some more wood, aren't we?" I asked.

"We'll need more after a while but don't touch that pile down in the ravine! If we use that we gotta replace it . . . That's somebody else's."

There was a long silence as we tended the fire. Finally Carl said: "Well, we made it." The fire softened up the old man. "You get yourself a job now—you'll be all set." He sounded like my father.

"You don't think it will be hard to find a job, do you? You said you thought there'd be plenty of work."

"Always is . . . I've always been able to find a job. If a guy's willing to work . . .

"Hope that other guy is here," Carl broke a silence that had lasted five minutes, "he owes me twenty dollars. I could use that! . . .

"It's good we got here early—now we got all day to plan ahead. Got to find out what the score is, see, you catch the bull local on the other side, over by that icehouse. But things change, they could be runnin' in the morning instead of the afternoon. You can't tell, and I'm glad we're here early so we can get set. Because this time tomorrow I want to be washing up to go to the employment office. It'll open about eight . . ."

The sun beamed over the horizon and the traffic began to flow on the roads into Wenatchee. "I've sat by these fires many a fuckin' night," Carl muttered, mostly to himself.

"But you said that in the old days you could find a jungle all cleaned up . . ."

"Yeah, that's right," he said, "just look at this pigpen."

"What do you plan on doing when the harvest is over? Just going to keep moving?"

"Me? I'm going up north to work, not to worry about what I'm goin' to do when I'm done workin'. No, I don't know where I'll go. I might stay here for the winter. If you want you're only off a little while. You pick crops after you're done pickin', then you're off for a while, and then you start prunin'. From pruning you go right into thinning. They work at least ten months a year here. Sixty-day vacation every year—that ain't bad. You can take a good trip—it's right at Christmas time."

We warmed our hands over the fire. The water boiled, breaking up an oily scum on its surface. "Christ," I said, "I'm glad that last one was a good ride. I needed a good ride after that sonofabitch coming into Spokane. That had to be one of the worst."

Carl interrupted: "Well, that was the train we should've caught in Minneapolis. Now you got to remember the number—seventy-seven—that comes here, and right into Seattle."

He scratched at his neck and said, "I gotta get this beard off—Christ, it's scratchin'! My hair's curly and it grows inward—it's a pain in the ass." He looked around the field. "Yeah, I like to get where they can see me, when I'm in these yards. And I have a club layin' ready." I hadn't noticed the stubby branch by his pack. "There's some camped over there, near the creek—mostly niggers, Indians. They wait and see if you're drunk—then they fuck with you. But one guy alone—with gear—he's in trouble, especially if he's drunk."

The water began to boil. Carl moved it to the unheated side of the grill, grasping the lip of the can between a wadded-up matchbook cover. He dug through his pack, found a rusty razor, a bar of soap, and an unbroken mirror. Soon he had a heavy lather on his face. He scratched and hacked away at his beard until his face was clean. "I'll bet you hardly recognize me! When I'm cleaned up I'm a different man!

"Here—you shave," he commanded, "or you go up the river alone. Ain't no excuse to look like hell when we got hot water and soap." I washed my face in the same water, lathered with the tramp's soap and shaved. I couldn't believe how good it felt to wash only three days' dirt away. The tramp seemed to read my mind. "It's good to wash up," he said softly. "It's been longer for me than for you." He dumped the water and put the shaving gear away.

"Now for breakfast!" I said, "How about some steak and eggs?"

"Shit," the tramp laughed, "beans. We eat our steak out of a can." We opened a can of beans and found the bread in the bottom of the pack. The tramp asked me if I'd like to have my bread toasted, then fashioned a holder out of a green branch, bending it back on itself just beyond a fork. The bread held firmly and the green branch did not burn. The tramp toasted four slices, browning both sides, before his holder finally gave way.

"Shouldn't we heat up those beans a little?" I asked.

"Beans are hard to heat in the can," he answered. "And if you heat 'em you got to eat them all." The tramp put the can in the coals and stirred the beans until they bubbled. We passed Carl's spoon back and forth until the beans were gone, then poured broth onto the last piece of toast.

"Good job," I said.

"Huh?"

"Good job on the toast—you didn't burn it."

He grunted, "If I had a wire, I could make it better—hell, I used to carry all this stuff with me. Shit, I carried everything—frying pan, oleo, eggs . . ."

"Eggs?"

"Sure, everything."

"You carried eggs on a freight train?"

"Goddamn right. Shit, that's easy. You just gotta wrap 'em."

"Wrap 'em? What in hell are you talking about?" But the tramp just looked around the field and said:

"I wonder if old fuckin' Woody's around. *He'd* give us some coffee—if he's got any. I expect we'll see guys around I know."

"We'll probably camp out tonight up the river, huh?" I said.

"Well, if we go to that Okanogan there's a shelter. But it's usually filled up. They got bunks—just springs and they're full of lice—damn near as good to sleep on the ground. Ain't much up there, it's a small town, a few stores, shoppin' area—that's about it. Farmer town—oh, there's a lot of bars—these towns up here got a lot of bars—for the working stiff. They got to get their money back you know. See, most of your pickers won't stay in Wenatchee—they come in and get out, up the valley to work. Cops are rough on you here and most of the tramps want to get out as soon as they can. This time of year most of them are going up to work. We ought to get there ourselves, by tonight—it's only eighty or ninety miles . . ."

I could see people rolling out from behind bushes at the edge of the ravine. Carl pointed to a man walking toward us:

"I wonder if that's Woody there now . . . No, by God, that looks like Crooked-Stem Smitty . . . I think it is! . . . Crooked-Stem!" he yelled to get the tramp's attention. "That's my fuckin' buddy!" He walked over to the figure and I heard him say: "That wouldn't be Crooked-Stem Smitty, now, would it? . . . No, fuck no, that's Boston Blackie! What the hell you doin' in from Pasco?" They walked toward me.

"I been here a long time," Blackie said. "What about you?"

"We just got in this morning," Carl answered.

Boston Blackie was a fat old man dressed in rumpled and oversized work clothes. He had a thick voice and he slurred his words like a drunk. He carried a sack and when he arrived at the fire I noticed his pink skin, watery eyes, and drooping eyelids. Half way into a speech he ceremoniously sat down, pausing to acknowledge me with a nod.

"Yeah, I been here a long time . . ." he said, "all went to the bottle!"

Carl interrupted. "I just got off the drunk! *He* met me in Minneapolis!" he said, nodding at me.

"They got thirty-three of them up there in jail," continued Blackie, "thirty-three. One goddamn-drunk-cocksucker from down there," he pointed to a building at the edge of the yard, "they let you take a shower and give you two sandwiches for three days—and all the coffee you want to drink in the meantime—plus a few donuts and sweet rolls . . . And that sonofabitch come down there, the other day—a tall, slim prick—he come runnin' in there drunk and says: 'I'm goin' to kill 'em all! . . . I'm goin' to *rush* 'em!' I was standin' there and I says, 'You better get away from me, you dirty cocksucker . . . You go ahead and rush us all and you'll be layin' dead on the floor, you son–of–a–bitch!' So they called the sheriff's department and it was two hours before they showed up. You can imagine the mess when they did!"

"They pickin' yet?" Carl interrupted.

"Yeah, that outfit I'm goin' to work for is startin'—I was supposed to start yesterday. But you know how it is sometimes—you ain't got anything wrong with you when you're loaded with booze, but after the booze dies off your teeth start hurtin' or something—then you're on the bunk . . ."

He began rummaging through his pack. "Well, I'll tell you what," he said, "I can furnish the coffee if you can furnish the water—how's that?"

"Good enough!" Carl answered.

"You know you gave me coffee when I didn't have none," Blackie said to Carl.

"I told you I'd run into someone I knew right away!" Carl said to me.

"Not very many you don't know," Blackie said. "Nine out of ten. But most of them are up in the valley already. There was thirty of them left on a freight last night goin' up."

Blackie took a dirty aluminum sauce pan from his sack and filled it with water. He put it on the fire and when it began to boil he threw in a large handful of coffee from a plastic bag. The most delicious of smells rose from the hobo camp. "Well, this here is regular grind, I don't know if you'll like that. *I* still prefer it to that newfangled freezed stuff."

"We ain't seen coffee since Minneapolis, and this kid has been complainin' all the way. I think he'd marry an old whore to get a cup!" Carl said.

Blackie laughed: "It's no good to travel without . . ."

After a minute, Blackie asked, "Preacher McCall and that bunch—seen them around?"

"They were up with me in Oroville," said Carl, "thinning."

The coffee was soon ready and Boston Blackie turned to me: "You need coffee cups?"

Carl nodded to me: "He might—I just found one layin' down by that creek." Blackie said:

"That's better than nothin' "; he handed me a brown plastic cup, the kind you'd see in an all-night diner, and said: "You can't drink out of your fucking hand!"

"We were just talking about coffee," said Carl, "he wanted to go all the way up town to get a cup!"

"Well, this'll cost you two bits!" Boston Blackie said seriously.

"You must be out of snouse," Carl said.

"That's just the way I treat new acquaintances." Blackie was chuckling as he poured the coffee.

"Yeah, you must be out of snouse. Blackie's got to have his Copenhagen, or he's a mean sonofabitch."

"No, no, I got my 'hagen." He poured the coffee carefully past the grounds that floated near the surface.

Carl turned to me: "Him and I was in a mission together in Pasco!"

"I was there last winter," Blackie said, "I took pneumonia there."

Carl interrupted: "I worked for that Earl Guillat. I could only stay with that fuckin' guy so long and that 'friend' of his, Steve. . . . I suppose he's still there . . ."

"Yeah, he's still there. I went lookin' for work in August and he said there weren't no work . . ."

"You could go camp-cooking, on a ranch. Shit, you cooked for all those guys in the mission!"

"Well, this time I was upstairs, down in bed for two weeks. They was carrying the soups up, everything for me to help out . . . Almost put me in the hospital. I pretty near died. Now I got that goddamn stomach deal on top of that . . ."

"I stayed in Minneapolis all winter," Carl said, "then I went to Montana with Woody."

"I herded sheep for John Drafus, out of Wolf Creek for two months," Blackie continued.

"I herded for John Cameron over there in Cascade," Carl answered. "Yeah, I was with old Crooked-Stem Smith there this spring. He ate me out of house and home!"

"That fella! Oh, Christ, everybody knows how he can eat!" Blackie rummaged through his sack and said, "You need some clothes?" Blackie was trying to unload stuff he didn't need. There seemed to be some unfinished business going on. Blackie held out a pair of ragged woolen pants. "These fit you?" he asked Carl.

"Oh, I got a couple pair . . ." Carl began.

"Christ, I got enough for all winter—I don't need these. Here, stand up and see." Carl stood up—the pants fell over his shoes. Then Carl turned to me, "Here, you take 'em." I could see he really enjoyed aiming Blackie's attention at me. Neither of us wanted the pants.

I told Blackie: "Well, I think I'm pretty loaded down . . . Thanks, though." He went on and on: "Where I'm going, I got these new jeans, warshed once; another pair, warshed once or twice . . . I won't have to tear up the ones I got on now, when I get to work."

Carl finally took Blackie's pants and stuffed them in his pack. He didn't want Boston Blackie's charity, that much was clear. "Yeah, I got to get to work," he mumbled to himself, "somebody's got to be pickin'!"

After a long break in the conversation Carl said, "You seen Woody around here? You know—that little guy."

Blackie answered: "No, he pulled out—they don't know where he went."

"I'll be damned!" Carl said and Blackie continued:

"He got a bad name. You get a bad name on the road and you get scared to go . . . Woody stayed all goddamn fuckin' winter in that old shack—never paid that man a nickel's worth of rent. Gettin' welfare, and the stamps every month—never paid that man a dime!"

"You know that guy that was with him with the black dog?" Carl asked.

"Yeah, Al. He caused trouble all over here—he even caused trouble with the Polack."

"He owes me twenty bucks!" Carl interrupted, "I loaned him twenty bucks last winter—that's the end of that!" Carl laughed and slapped his knee like it was all a big joke. He'd been bitching about his twenty bucks for three days. Blackie ignored him and continued:

"He was stayin' over there with Woody and everything was goin' pretty good . . . I went over to that grocery store and that lady said: 'Hey, Blackie, I'd like to get two apple pickers . . .' "; Blackie made his voice sound like a crochety old lady; ". . . and I says: 'I'm sorry little lady, I can't pick your apples now because I got to go up to Branches the ninth' . . . 'Then go and find me some apple pickers, Blackie!' . . . I came down and told Woody and Al: 'You fellas want to pick apples for that lady that works in the grocery store? Four acres she has to pick, payin' six dollars a bin—go right over and see her.' Well, they went right over and talked to her. 'Yeah, you bet, okay'—the usual bullshit. So they go to work pickin', stayed sober four or five days of pickin' and then the next thing you know Al got drunk; they all got drunk. Al took a high-powered rifle and shot—the old Polack was in his shack, but he was in the back sittin' on his toilet—coffee pot sittin' on his electric hot plate—and BANG! BANG! Al shot right through the fuckin' window, shot the coffee pot all to hell; shot right through the ceiling . . .

"And they had another big scrape. Polack laid Al's head open with an axe, cut him down his face—sheriff had to get him. They found blood on the floor at the Polack's and saw the Polack layin' in bed, drunk, and that sheriff said, 'You might as well come along too' . . . Yeah, they had nothin' but trouble over there. Now Dutch Shorn is livin' there with that Big George. And over there, up in that area there—that's where I am sleepin' these days."

Carl interrupted: "I won't sleep in these yards at night!"

Blackie ignored him: "Dutch's got a three-room house, and McLure got a three-room shack, but I don't go in with them. I go in and drink coffee, maybe warsh my hands and shave or somethin'— 'bout all. I don't ask for anything to eat, if they offer it to me, I don't want it."

"Causes trouble," Carl said.

"I don't want any," Blackie continued, "because I don't want to be under obligation. Not that I would be, far as they're concerned 'cause they've known me for years—they'd do anything in the world to help me."

Carl asked, "How much they payin' this year?"

"I haven't found out. I worked in the summer apples between Pateros and Brewster. I drove tractor. Two dollars an hour. They pay the pickers ten dollars a bin for pickin' them apples. An' that crooked-nose Polack, he was there—he picked. Old Mike and me was together there seven days last week—jungle in Pateros. But there aren't many of them. I been sittin' around here three or four days. Some of them did go up and pick a few yesterday—for two dollars an hour. But that's color pickin'—I don't do it."

The lull lasted minutes. Finally, Carl said: "By God, I finally got me a good sleeping bag! Sonofabitch cost me forty-five dollars!" Blackie wasn't interested. "You need it up in this country," Carl added.

"They like to steal a packsack, something like that one," Blackie answered, "I'll sleep in these here blankets."

Carl looked down at the club beside Boston Blackie's gear, "Fuckin' old two-by-four ain't worth a shit."

"Oh, them Mexican cocksuckers . . ."

"Course it is some wood. If you could catch them messin' around."

"Yeah, well, I'm gettin' too old for that shit," Blackie said, "too fuckin' old to be messin' with some jackroller tryin' to take my gear off me. I'd rather not have any. That way I got nuthin' to worry about . . ."

"Well, I helped with all the thinnin' and all the proppin'," Blackie continued after a minute, "an' I worked in the summer apples, drivin' tractor—five hundred and eighty-four dollars after I paid for all my groceries out of the grocery store. Bars of candy and tobaccee I bought. Lasted three days in Brewster."

"Three days!" Carl sucked his cheeks in like he was surprised. But Blackie continued: "An' I know so goddamn fuckin' many of them—sitting around here hungry and broke, sick, heads down in the goddamn bar in the mornin': 'Hel-lo Blackie, Christ I'm glad you came in . . .' 'Yeah, you betcha . . .' Last spring I stayed seventeen days in a hotel. Four dollars and twenty cents a night! That was in Brewster, and I was drunk every day . . ."

"You know that Old Bill that used to hang aroung there? Wonder what ever happened to him . . . he was gone this spring—somewhere in a hospital I heard."

"I dunno . . . I ain't seen *him* in a long time . . ."

"Shit," said Carl, "he got over four hundred dollars a month pension!"

"Well, little Duffy—he died, you know," Blackie said, "died in a hospital in Brewster . . . Laid up five days unconscious."

If Carl heard the tramp, he didn't show it. "That Brewster country ain't a bad country to work in . . . I been up there a lot lately . . ."

Blackie interrupted. "There's only one thing about gettin' off in Brewster. You have the door open on both sides and you watch him. When that engineer jumps off of them engines—on the head end—and starts to run to get that mail—you got to throw everything off; you got to hit the ground! Soon as he runs and gets that mail and jumps back on that diesel-*high*ball—he'll push that throttle back and run like a son-of-a-bitch—you got to fly out of that car! And you know damn well after you throw everything on the ground he's goin' much too fast to get off!"

Carl laughed. "Yeah, right there by Campbell's orchard."

"That's it!" said Blackie. "I was there for a week drunk, too. Dusty, that bunch. I was up there with old Mike. We was sleepin' under trees . . . We'd get up and go across in the mornin', see if they needed anybody. Finally left—caught the fuckin' bus that comes from Brewster to Pateros and stayed in the fuckin' willows there—way up the other end where they load them chips."

Carl interrupted. "Yeah, I used to be up there—good jungle there."

"We stayed seven days . . ." Blackie's speech was punctuated by a searing, tubercular-sounding cough, "You're layin' around a place, warshin' up, cleanin' up and cookin'—restin'—you know, seven days in one jungle gets to be a long time! I was walkin' around . . . walkin' around . . . Mike says, 'What's the matter? . . . I know,' he says, 'I'm surprised you even stayed here three days.' I decided to take a ride. 'Where you goin'?' he asked me. 'I'm goin' to Wenatchee.' So by God here comes the train—he didn't run on Labor Day, or Sunday. So on Tuesday here he comes—ninety-two cars, I counted them. 'Jesus Christ,' I told Mike, 'I'm goin' to break if I don't go to Wenatchee tonight . . . they're goin' to set off the head end over here, and I'm goin' to get a lift down.' We're sittin' and sittin' and here comes the train, by God he sets off the front end just like I said. See, I had asked the braky, 'You goin' to take that stuff to Wenatchee?' He says, 'All that stuff, twenty-two cars goin' back to Wenatchee.' I says, 'Jesus

Christ Almighty, they're goin' to take all that shit down to Wenatchee!' So I got my train and Mike says: 'I'll take the bus tomorrow mornin' and I'll go to Antiat, or some goddamn place.' 'I know where you're going—right back to Brewster. Six in the mornin', seven-thirty, you'll be sittin' in the bar lookin' for a drink . . . I know . . . I know all about it. You ain't goin' to no Antiat *now*!' " He coughed, shaking back and forth until his eyes watered. Finally he wiped his eyes with his shirt-tail, exposing his fat belly, and continued: "We didn't do much work this time. You know we had a hundred-five two weeks straight, up here in this country? Hundred and five—it never dropped below eighty. And yesterday, at twelve the sheriff people were comin' down. I says, 'It's awful warm, lady,' 'Yeah,' she says, 'It's eighty-two degrees back in my *house*' "

We were dry and the story had run out. "Well, get your cups," Blackie said. "We got some more coffee brewin'." The coffee went around again. "I don't know if it's the kind that suits you . . . I don't make it strong enough, then the next fuckin' time it's too strong."

"It's been a long time since I had coffee," Carl said.

"It's strong and black—just the way I like it," I said when Blackie looked toward me.

"I just switched to this regular ground up in Pateros," he continued. "I can't make it to suit everybody. If I make it too strong and offer them coffee, they say, 'Christ Almighty, it's too strong!' 'Well, then put some water in it!' "

"If they don't like it then they got no business drinkin' it," Carl said, then added as he filled his cup, "I got to get up the valley to get something goin'. That's what I'm tryin' to make up my mind on. See, he's never worked up there—and I know people in both towns, but I don't know if we should go to Okanogan or Brewster. I worked pretty near all summer up in Oroville, but that's so goddamn hard to get into. You got to call from Okanogan and they'll come and get you—if they need you."

"Well," Blackie said, "if you want to pick for Jack Nichols, he's got six different orchards."

"Yeah, but they say he ain't much good to work for."

"Treated me alright," Blackie said, "very nice man. You know some of these people that knocks the other man . . ."

Carl interrupted. "Ain't no good their self. A lot of guys say they won't work for Stutterin' Jack, but he was all right by me."

"Most of them people, most of them fellas," Blackie said, "don't believe in 'live and let live.' The reason Jack Nichol's no good is because they want wine in the camp, and they want to raise hell and smash everything up, see. Well, you can't have that around a group of men. There's a certain percentage of men who want to make a dollar out of it—and plan to stay all the way through the harvest. Well, the other one comes in there, fallin' over the beds fightin' and everything—well, he destroys it for the one that is sober. An' naturally, the drinkin' man can't stand him."

"No, fuck no," Carl agreed.

"I can't be around 'em," Blackie said.

Carl interrupted again, "I can't be around a sober man when I'm drunk, that I know."

Blackie agreed again. "When I'm around a sober man when I'm drunk, I got to go away from that man. And it don't matter how long I knew him or anything. Yesterday mornin' I came down here walkin' on that side of the bridge, and there they were. Three six-packs. 'Oh, Blackie, come on over . . .' One fella came runnin' over carrying three bottles and two dollars for another bottle, 'How's everything Blackie!' I says 'What the hell is *this*? You ain't goin' to get Blackie drunk! *I* ain't goin' to get drunk with you!' So with the two dollars—I bought some beans and bread. I could go without going to a fuckin' store to buy their bottle!"

Another train rolled in from the east. Five tramps jumped from a flatcar as it idled through the yards. "Coming in for food stamps," Carl said, "look at 'em all—cold as a sonofabitch!"

"Wenatchee seems to be the place," I said, "I was comin' out of Seattle last year on a boxcar full of guys and they all jumped to Wenatchee to get stamps."

"Well," Blackie replied, "I ain't goin' to bitch about it. Because all through cherry pickin' time and peach pickin' time—thirty-six dollars worth. Regular as a clock I get myself a book of thirty-six."

"Well, we could have stopped in Sandpoint—was it yesterday? And got in to Newport—thirty-six dollars right there," Carl added.

"You could have got them in Newport—not many questions asked." Blackie continued: "Don't have to go through too much rigamarole. All you do is get off in Sandpoint and catch that local down—he leaves you off in front of the depot—the Milwaukee depot. Great Northern nearby—all you got to remember is to go right over a few tracks to catch back. You sign up one day and the next day you go to the post office—get your vouchers for your stamps, go into the city police headquarters and the little girl in there—one or the other of the little ladies in there—will give you the stamps—but the next thing is—get the hell out of there. That can be the big problem."

Carl agreed. "That local ain't runnin' much any more . . ."

We sat quietly around the fire. I was drowsy from Blackie's stories and the heat of the sun, low in the eastern sky. Carl dug through his pack—the food had shifted to his gear—and pulled out a can of beans. But before he offered our food to Blackie he looked over at me. "I ain't hungry," I said, "but why don't you open 'em up and share 'em with Blackie!" Carl turned to the tramp: "We got some beans here, Blackie, you hungry?"

The tramp surprised me by saying: "Don't believe so, Carl, I got a couple slices of bread in here . . ." Carl went ahead and opened the beans and when they were bubbling hot he offered them again. This time Blackie accepted, and they finished them off, passing the spoon back and forth.

"That train up the branch still leaves the same time, don't it?" Carl asked when the beans were finished.

"Yeah—between three and five o'clock. Fella can go right down there to the shelter—one o'clock or five after one, and get free sandwiches. That's three days straight and you can sleep on one of their army cots if you want. You get a good sandwich in there, plenty of scalding hot water, good shower, towel . . . You can fix yourself up real good for the train ride— that's if a fella *wants* it. I 'preciate a place like that because you can do some good for yerself."

"What kind of a sandwich do they give you?" Carl asked.

"Oh, some peanut butter, jelly, or some tunafish—maybe some baloney. I like that, see that's what I done when I got back. In fact, I took a shower yesterday. Christ, they furnish the razor, after-shave lotion; I got all cleaned up. That's awful nice down there—I 'preciate it. Of course some of these men I know getting pensions sayin', 'They're ruinin' the country down there. . . .' I say 'What the fuck you talkin' about, ruinin' the country? It couldn't be ruined any more than it is already!' 'Cause they got a full gut, dollar in their pocket—this kind of a place is no good! I see one of them, he still comes down and has a sandwich an' a cup of coffee. I gave him hell.

48

'How are you, Blackie.' I says, 'I'm alright. *You* got three hundred dollars a month comin' in, what the goddamn hell do you have to come down here and take the stuff from the stiffs?' He says, 'Fuck you, streamline!' 'Don't worry about it,' I says, 'It's pretty fuckin' cheap when you gotta come down and take the bread and butter from the tramp tryin' to go out on a fuckin' old job!' Sittin' around there drinkin' coffee, bullshittin' . . . By God, come to think of it this ain't a bad cup of coffee either!"

"Good," I answered, "very strong."

"Yeah, well, I get so dee-sgusted with myself," Blackie said out of the blue, "I don't know what to do. I can have a hundred dollars this mornin' . . ."

Carl interrupted, "An' you won't have a dime tomorrow—I know, I know. I'm the same way." Carl nodded at me; "Well, when you saw me I was drinking a quart of Grand Canadian, wasn't I?"

"Yeah, that you were."

"That's pitiful," Blackie said seriously; "you ought to be ashamed of yourself. But who's kidding who—it's the same with me." He looked Carl straight in the eye and bent forward to emphasize his point: "Several times lately I found myself wonderin'—just what the hell's going to become of me!" They began to laugh, and they laughed and laughed; I thought they'd roll on the ground. Then Carl said: "I had a dollar, and a few pennies left—that's all I had left from that last job. Here I am, couple of days later, fucked up on an old freight train!"

"Last time I found you over there in Laurel," Blackie began again, "summer of '73. You were in hell of a shape that time. You wouldn't even talk. I tried to talk to you that mornin' but you couldn't even say 'Good Mornin', Blackie.' You was tryin' to shave. Man, you was doin' some goddamn stunts—Je-sus, that razor was bouncin'! I took a long look and I says to myself: 'Well, don't be bullshittin' with old Carl now. He's sure as hell sick. He don't want to hear no story about what happened over there, or who's comin' in here . . .' " Blackie began chuckling, "you were on a hell of a goddamn drunk!"

"Right there," Carl said, "right here in Laurel around those same buildings where we waiting for a train!"

Blackie continued: "Fellow went with me last year—just a hell of a good friend of mine. He's an ex-sailor, lived in that-there Seattle—he

49

gets a good pension. Just a hell of a good fellow. He came down here and I was sittin' on the porch of that shack. 'So what do you want to do?' he says, as he was shakin' hands with me. 'What do you want to do this mornin', eat or drink?' I said, 'Oh oh oh—I can't figger out right away, I just got up!' 'If I know you, it won't take long for you to figure it out!' I took him up and got him a job at 'Custon Two'—we didn't have to work that afternoon, so we had dinner and supper, and breakfast, and went to work. I was drivin'—and he was pickin'.

"So my buddy, that poor fella, got one bin picked and he is standin' there lookin'. I drove the tractor around there and says, 'Well you got two bins ahead of you to fill.' 'Yes,' he says, 'and I already got trouble—lost my goddamn glasses and I can't make those tickets out.' See, you've got to fill out tickets when you fill a bin," Blackie said to Carl. "So my buddy lost his glasses. I ain't got time to be lookin' in the grass—who knows where in the hell he lost 'em. Naturally, if he knew where he lost 'em he'd go get 'em! 'Son–of–a–bitch,' I says, 'lost your glasses!' We're down there by the tracks and he's thinkin' about that local comin'. 'Blackie, let's get on that train and go back to Wenatchee.' So he's comin' and comin' and he slows down like he does to get the mail, and by god, we caught back! Left our stuff right there in that orchard!"

Blackie looked at Carl and said: "Well, we been at this a long time—it ain't nothin' new to you or me."

Carl nodded and grunted: "No, no, fuck no . . ."

"There ain't no excitement in it to me any more," Blackie continued. "Fella was with me last summer, comin' out of Minneapolis—and he was worried about the jungles. 'Shit!' I said, 'you don't have to worry about the jungles—main thing to worry about is something to put in the kettles and fryin' pans I'm carryin' here!' We had a bunch of sardines, bread and crackers. We rode along drinkin' water, eatin', and as he was ridin' along he says to me: 'By God, the scenery looks good along the tracks!' 'Full stomach,' I says, layin' my head on the bedroll—*I* knew what was ahead. Next mornin' I'm waitin' to hear what he has to say. We're ridin', and he's standin', lookin', lookin', hands in his pockets, an' scratchin' his head every once in a while. Pretty soon I says: 'You ain't got no sardine, no fuckin' bread, nuthin' to drink—how does she look out there now? How she lookin' out there today?' 'Ahhh Blackie,' he says, 'no good!' 'I know,' I says, 'empty gut!' "

Carl chuckled.

"Nice to have a little sack of groceries," Blackie added, "makes that scenery look darn nice!"

He turned to me. "Well, I've known that fellow Carl a long time and he always gave me a bite when I was hungry—a smoke when I was short. And I seen many a one he shared his coffee with."

"See what I told you?" Carl said to me, "I told you I'd meet somebody . . . Always do . . ."

"Many a drink of wine, many a drinkin' fool," Blackie said, "that's our way of livin'—that's the way we got to go along . . ."

"If he's a tramp I'll give anything I got," Carl said, "and there's some I won't even say 'Good morning' to . . ."

I had begun to drowse off when a tall, thin tramp ambled over to the jungle. Blackie greeted him jovially: "Well, good morning there, George!" George was weaving back and forth. Blackie looked him over carefully and said: "Ahhh, George, you better have a shot of coffee—you look like hell!"

"What did you do to my friend Woody?" Carl asked. "Somebody must have run him out of the country."

George was slurring his words and stuttering and stammering. "What d-d-did *I* do wish him? He runs himshelf out . . ."

"That figgers," Carl said. "And I'd like to run into that Al, too. I gave him twenty bucks! He was supposed to come to Minneapolis—he never showed. I was here—Christ, I had over five hundred dollars—I made five-sixty-eight in a little over two weeks in Oroville thinnin' this year . . . I made good . . ." George coughed and spat. He looked sick and dizzy as he swayed back and forth. But Carl ignored him, and continued, "Took the bus from here all the way back to Minni'. That Al still got his dog?"

George answered: "Yeah, he left everything but his dog. The last we heard from him he was over in Troy—But I wouldn't believe it."

"Well, he used to stay in Troy," Carl said. "On the other side of the tunnel. That jungle, er . . . that dump! That's years ago, though . . ."

Blackie rearranged the branches and charred two-by-fours to get the fire going again. George watched him with a dopey smile.

"What's the matter, George, haven't you ever seen this before? Don't you know how to build a jungle?"

"No-oo."

Carl interrupted: "Ask a stupid question—" Blackie laughed, and Carl said: "Well, I've seen guys so helpless they couldn't do it!"

"Oh, there's some like that, but not our buddy George!"

"Well, I think I built some of those," George said.

"I ain't goin' to go that far myself," Carl answered.

"You heard me say I think I could build a jungle," George repeated. "If I don't fuck up, I could probably get it right . . ."

Carl looked over at him: "There's got to be a seat around here somewhere, George. I'd let you sit on my bedroll but the sonofabitch is too dirty. I don't know if you've seen one like this . . ." He picked up the bag and handed it to George. "Here, feel this special material."

"Yeah, that's one of those fancy nylons," George mumbled.

"You know how much this thing cost me? Forty-five dollars!"

"Good God!" said Blackie.

"I can't stand it in this kind of weather," Carl continued, "it's too warm. But hell, I can sleep out in the winter with it! If I keep it that long."

Blackie tossed a few pieces of cardboard to George, telling him to sit down and drink his coffee.

Blackie rummaged through his pack and produced a small, turquoise-colored transistor radio. He turned the volume up all the way and pulled out the aerial, but all he could get was static. He put the radio on a piece of iron railing, and then twiddled the nobs until a station came in faintly. The other tramps watched without comment.

"Can't beat this kind of radio," Blackie bragged. "I got it for nothing and fixed it up with this cardboard back. Now she sounds purty as hell."

"You know they stole my good radio," Carl said, "that forty-dollar one."

52

Blackie ignored him and continued: "I'm going to hook a lantern battery to this—I got the battery and all the connections."

The sound faded from the radio and the tramp put it back into his pack. Blackie coughed and spat. "Well, you fellas got enough coffee? Go ahead—fill your pouch up with tobacco—go ahead and help yourself—if you ain't got a pouch put it in something else . . . You got any matches?"

"Yeah, goddammit, I got a whole carton!" Carl muttered.

Blackie began jabbering at Carl, trying to convince him to take some tobacco or coffee—anything at all. Carl finally agreed: "Well, Blackie, I guess I better get some coffee for my buddy here—he was all out of sorts this morning without his coffee."

"Better take enough to last all day—and the ride up the branch!"

Carl dug into the sack. "This is tobacco! I thought you said coffee!"

"Christ, that right? Well, I can give you coffee, if you want!"

They began all over again. Carl refused, then finally accepted small amounts of both coffee and tobacco. Then he quickly changed the subject.

"I think I wore out my welcome in Minneapolis for a while. I owe Joe's Liquor Store seventy dollars. Besides spending all the money of my own, I still got Louis's keys from the market—I'll have to send them back. That's the second time I've done that and he ain't going to appreciate it!"

I washed my plastic cup and handed it to Blackie, thanking him with a short "Much obliged."

"Oh, you can have that cup!" Blackie said. I began to refuse but Carl stopped me: "You better keep it or you'll just have to get one somewhere else."

Blackie said he had another one in his pack, but he added, pointing to the cup he'd lent me: "I carried that there one five years."

"You sure you want to part with it?"

"No, no—I got another one . . . Man's got to have a cup to drink his coffee with."

"You know that's what us oldtimers do," Carl said, "we get together—'Well, you got this,' or 'You got that,' . . . Before you know it everybody's got something."

Blackie added: "But if a man's going to be on the road, he should have his own fryin' pan, plate, spoon, fork—"

53

Carl interrupted: "Mine's in Oroville—"

"Because what the hell," Blackie continued, "I don't appreciate carryin' a whole lot of shit for somebody else—hell, I'm not going to do it! I'm too old, too old to be carryin' a lot of shit for somebody else!"

"My stuff is all in Oroville," Carl repeated. "You know those little iron pans? I got one of those, and I got some that tinware—coffee pot, little saucepan, utensils . . ."

"That's right," Blackie said, "you ought to carry it. You never know what's going to happen on a freight train. He may have a wreck and be there for days. No water jug—nuthin' to eat—Jesus Christ Almighty you'll be in a hell of a shape! Happened to me more times than I'd care to recall."

Men kept appearing from behind bushes. They'd stretch, smooth out their rumpled clothes, assemble what gear they had and walk away toward the shelter. I'd seen none of them an hour before as I'd walked through the field; now it seemed they were sprouting from the land itself.

"Look at them all," Carl said, "heading for that place over there. Don't anybody jungle up proper no more?"

"Ain't that many places left," Blackie said. "Can't stay there—all you can do is sit and eat those two sandwiches for three days! Three nights lodging—then you gotta go! And they're really on a rampage around here. You can't jungle around here no more! Jesus Christ, they tore all those big trees down there where the cabooses used to be. Tore out that water cooler—chased us all the hell out of there. That's where I had my jungle—I'd make my coffee, wash, shave, then I'd set around that big shade tree. Well, Christ, one morning I slept in. I woke up about nine—here comes that bulldozer rattling! 'What the hell is this?' I says, 'They going to bulldoze us? Get our fucking luggage,' I says to my buddy, 'that bulldozer's coming right at us! Get our fucking luggage—we ain't goin' to jungle *here* no more!' . . .

"And that was a nice place, a real nice place. They took the cabooses clear up town, cut those trees down. Reason was fellas was breakin' in those fuckin' cabooses. Kickin' the doors in. So they got dee-sgusted with it and they tore the hell out of everything. Wenatchee ain't the town it used to be—they're makin' it goddamn hard for the man trying to go out on a goddamn job."

54

Carl wandered off with George to find some eyeglasses George said he'd stashed. I told Blackie about our trip across Montana on bull locals and he commented: "When a man's on the road he gets a rabbit in his ass—he's in a big fucking hurry. He gets to the next jungle and he's on the bum anyway—it don't make much difference." Blackie heated water to wash. When he'd finished he said: "Well, if Carl hadn't been all 'rum-drum' he'd a been on the right trains. 'Cause he knows what trains to catch. But like he said, he was probably sicker than hell, not knowing what the hell he's doing—*rum*-drummed. Oh, I been that way more times than I'd care to remember . . . livin' along the fuckin' tracks is no good . . . it just ain't no good."

I didn't know what to say. After a minute I said there were parts of the experience I liked and Blackie quickly interrupted: "You're young. When you get to be fifty-eight years old and have running around for thirty years, it won't be no fun any more. It was awfully exciting to me when I first started—when I first started, years ago—'31, '32, '33. Man, I was in the prime of my pride! Jesus Christ, I'd go up to a house: 'Good morning, good morning . . . Do you have a sandwich, something to eat?' 'Yeah, you betcha!' I was young then—it all looked good to me . . .

"If I stay outside this winter it'll be twenty-one winters outside—packsack and bedroll. It was different in them old days—in the steam engine days we rode the rods. Layin' down there underneath on a grain board or somethin'—you had to balance on those rods under the car. It wasn't an easy ride, but it wasn't a bad ride either—them trains went quite a bit slower.

"But after you go through all that it ain't no good no more. I'm too old—trains too fast now and I git hurt on some of those rides. Been at it too long . . ."

We both became silent. Blackie seemed lost in his reminiscences.

After thirty or forty minutes Carl and George returned, and Carl was wearing a pair of glasses.

"They work?" Blackie asked.

"They're bifocals, but I can read out of the bottom part," Carl answered.

"Well, that's good," Blackie said. "A lot better than nothing at all."

"Can't see shit out of the top section, though . . . I can see way in the distance—that's all. You know what I did? Took my glasses off and laid them on the bar. I was reading something. I always got the habit of laying them down, instead of stickin' them back in my pocket. I can do with these until I get somethin' better . . ."

George sat down on one of the cans. "How's your rope?" Carl asked. George didn't hear him. "How's your rope—do you need any rope?" Carl repeated.

"Rope?" George answered. "I guess I got what I need back in the shack."

"You need any different rope? I got this whole goddamn clothesline! Same as I got here." Carl lifted his sleeping bag, tied with a piece of rope, for George to see. I told Carl he'd better not give the rope away or we wouldn't have anything to dry out clothes on. "It ain't funny when you see guys that don't even have no bedroll rope," Carl said.

Blackie interrupted: "I been in that shape and it ain't no good. But now I'm set—I got two pair of pants on and a bedroll up there."

"Well, I just threw this stuff together—it was so goddamned dark out and I was drunk," Carl mumbled.

"And down below here," Blackie continued, ignoring Carl, "I got two of the finest pair of long-john thermoes, extry heavy! A whole boxload of them came in—a great big boxload!" Carl was definitely interested.

"You did! You got them down there?"

"Oh, they got all kinds of clothes down there. Christ almighty, jackets and socks, and everything."

"I ain't got no coat," Carl reflected.

"Well, Jesus Christ, I was sittin' there and here comes that big box. They set it down and I took a look. 'Say,' I says, 'could I have a look at those thermoes.' The lady says, 'Oh, they're not too—' 'Never mind, lady, they'll suit me just fine!' So I got one pair. Then they changed shifts and I says to that other fella that came on the second shift: 'Hey, could I get a pair of those thermoes?'—'Sure!' he says. So I got myself two pair, rolled up in that bedroll, Brand new! Damn, they'd cost fourteen, fifteen dollars a pair. Big, thick goddamn bastards. I saw them and I says to myself: 'Blackie, you might as well get them before winter—if you wait until winter, you might just have to go without!'"

"Did you see that suit I had last winter?" Carl asked. "I had aircorps flight pants—big-hooded jacket and underneath was a vest. A down vest and those felt boots."

"I saw you there in that yard last winter," Blackie recollected; "you were going to the grocery store to get a half of a gallon for you and that fella."

"Oh, yeah," Carl mumbled, "Al was there and Woody and I."

Blackie continued: "You was so goddamn drunk you didn't even recognize us. I never said nuthin' to you—I just looked. I said, 'You're so goddamn fuckin' drunk . . .' "

"Yeah, and I tried to get on that train," Carl said.

" 'You were so goddamn drunk,' I says, 'Look at him!' "

"You ought to have seen me that next day—sick. And I went to work. Went to work sick!"

"Didya ever get your half gallon, Carl?" Blackie asked seriously.

"Yeah, oh yeah, I got that half gallon. Woody and Al and the guy I was with. I can't remember his name . . ."

"I was sittin' there," Blackie continued, "what the hell did he call me? Smitty, that's it, Smitty."

"I was probably looking for Pipestone Smitty," Carl said.

"I didn't say a fuckin' thing," Blackie repeated. "I just looked—I says to myself, 'He's so fuckin' drunk he don't know who the hell I am.' You says, 'I'll bring the half gallon back!' "

"You brought that half gallon back?—I was surprised you could even walk. I got up and left before you came back. Dee-sgusting!" Blackie coughed and spit.

"God, I was sick the next day!" Carl said. "Oh, Jesus! Sick heavin', drink of water; up it'd come. I was so sick I thought I was goin' to die . . . You get so sick, you wish you could." After a long pause, Carl added, quietly: "Yeah, I should stop that old shit.

"I went up to Hiland Orchard," he continued, "lasted three and a half days. He started me at two dollars an hour, prunin', then he changed me from two dollar an hour, to fifty cents a tree. Why—that cheap sonofabitch! He hired me at two dollars an hour and then changed me once I was workin'. 'Well, you're pretty good at that,' he says, 'I'm going to let you go by the tree!' It was about a dollar ten cents an hour by the tree.

"I couldn't do that job fast—that's hard work; it's hard on your arms. Some of those cock-suckin' trees is as big as that willow"; Carl

57

pointed to a tree that must have been forty feet high. Blackie looked at him and snickered.

"You sure, Carl? That willow's a pretty big tree!"

"Well, maybe not quite that big. All I know is that I was standin' on top of a twelve-foot ladder—standing on the top of that sonofabitch reaching up with a 'loper . . .'"

Blackie had begun to pack his gear. He turned to us: "Well, I'm going to go down there—you know where them trees is on the other side of the building? That's where I'm going to be sitting in the shade." Carl said we might be by. I thanked Blackie for the coffee and the cup and he answered graciously: "Oh, don't worry about that!"

"Okay, Blackie," Carl said, "we may be over in a while."

"Well, you might as well come on over and get those two sandwiches . . . Plenty of coffee there to drink; with cream and sugar—well, it's that powered milk and sugar. And he'll go up the branch this afternoon about four—or chree-churdy. I'd walk up from that end where they've put those cabooses—that's the way I'm going."

When he'd gone, Carl said: "Well, that's Boston Blackie. I ate his ass out because he was always bumming my coffee and he would never come up with any. Finally, I told him I'd had enough of his shit and you see how quick he offered coffee this morning!"

"He seemed like a nice enough guy to me," I answered.

"Yeah, well, he ain't so good as you think. A lot of guys hate his guts. And if you associate with him they won't associate with you. In the winter time you'll find him right in a mission—he even said he spent last winter in the Pasco mission."

"He said he was sick, for Christ sake! He's sick now—didn't you hear him cough?"

"He ain't sick. That's what he says. He's a bullshit artist. But I've given him so fuckin' much I don't feel like giving him no more. See, he's piecin' me out of a little bit of tobacco, coffee—it'll cost me a five-dollar bill to pay him back! By the time he gets done, it'll cost me a five-dollar bill!

"See, he's a regular packsack tramp," Carl continued, "he's carried a pack ever since I've known him."

"Would you call him a bindle stiff then?"

"Well, no . . . A packsack tramp. We don't call nobody bindle stiffs—that's old-time talk. Bindle stiff is a guy that carries a whole bunch of little packages—gunny sacks, shit like that. They're oldtimers. They carry pots and pans, everything they need to cook up proper in. And if they find a good pan, or pot—they'll put in the sack even if they don't need it. You'll see them loaded down, two, three sacks full."

"Well, I don't know, Carl," I said, "I don't know what kind of a man Blackie is. But I know that coffee will taste good tomorrow morning about four or so when I start shivering and wiping the dew off my face."

"Yeah, you're right. You'll get cold. But it won't be the first time, and it probably won't be the last.

"See, what Blackie wanted was for somebody to go down there with him for protection. He knows them on the prowl won't fuck with him if there's more than one—and nobody'll jungle with old Blackie no more . . ." He yawned in the mid-morning sun and stretched. "Yeah, that Blackie, he's quite a guy. I don't know what the fuck I'm going to do with them pants. Put them on when I wash the rest of them, I suppose."

A man with clean overalls and an engineer's hat walked along the tracks and then suddenly veered in our direction.

"I think that's a bull," Carl said.

"Think we ought to pack up?"

"We might. We'll do what he says. He might run us over to the other side."

We gathered our gear and moved toward a ravine near the edge of the yard. As we were moving away the man in clean overalls again abruptly changed directions and returned to the tracks.

There were two tramps sitting around a fire. The older of the two looked at Carl as we walked up and said: "It's a long day across that damn hump, isn't it?"

"Three long days," Carl said. "You just come over too?"

"Yeah, I came out of Minneapolis about two weeks ago—almost rode that mail train. I was tryin' to get on that ninety-seven and I got myself tangled up with six or seven goddamn hippies! Two *girls*, two fuckin' dogs, and a goddamn bicycle! In a boxcar! Well, I didn't know it until I jumped in thar—I was stuck in Chicago and that damn yard is no place to be so I says, 'I'm going to ride this sonofabitch to St. Paul anyway!' Next morning we get to St. Paul—they had never rode

59

a freight before—and some of them wanted to go to Spokane and some were goin' to Seattle. Wanted me to ride on out and show them the ropes—shit, I thought maybe I can *eat* off them! . . .

"They started talking"; Carl and I had dropped our gear and reclined against some rocks. "They started talking," the tramp repeated, " 'We got to stop and rest for a while—we can't ride four days without rest!'—hell, none of them looked like they was over twenty-five years old. So we got to St. Paul and they was standin' in the door lookin' and some goddamn bitch called the bull. Wouldn't you know it—fuckin' bull comes down and run us all off! I've been riding that sonofabitch for years and that St. Paul bull never fucked with me. So this little boy says: 'I'm going to ride to town, get a cab, and go over to Minneapolis to catch him.' 'Yeah,' I answered, 'If you can get a *cab* to the yard you can catch him real easy.' I took off and crawled up in the weeds and went to sleep.

"I don't know where they went. I woke up later and saw that mail train and almost caught him, but I saw all them piggybacks and realized that wasn't no freight train."

"I rode him once," Carl interrupted. "I got on that sonofabitch and I didn't go fifteen miles and I wished I was off! That sonofabitch tore like a bastard! When I got to Minot I says never, never again!"

"I caught ninety-seven in the middle of the night," the tramp continued, "and I left my hippie friends behind. That's a lot of bullshit? They got money—that ridin' is just for fun. They smoke that marijuana—girls, dogs, all piled on a freight—now I suppose that St. Paul yard will be hot for a while.

"I didn't think this harvest was goin' to get going for a while and I had this cocksucker," he nodded to his silent companion, "with me all the way from Spokane, so I took him to Newport and camped out a little over three weeks on the riverbank, pretty near a mile out of town. Newport is such a little fuckin' town if you cross the fuckin' street you're in I-dee-hoe. You got to be careful—if you ever stop there to get your foodstamps, tell 'em you're stayin' down in the Milwaukee hotel. Don't tell them nothing else—you might be tellin' them you're stayin' in I-dee-hoe—and then there won't be no foodstamps!

"We got our foodstamps and we was walkin' up the tracks gettin' ready to catch that local over to Sandpoint and some young boy—big sonofabitch, and this prick was dressed up a little bit and he had a bunch of pencils in his pocket—comes up to us. He says to me: 'Are you Charlie West?' I says, 'Hell, no.' I don't know what the fuck they were huntin' for, or how they got his name. Then he asked me, 'You know any place they sell foodstamps in this town?' And I says, 'Well, I dunno, I heard some tramps say you could sell 'em in a beer joint somewhere, but I dunno; don't ask me!' He says, 'You got any to sell?' And I says, 'Hell, no!'—he wasn't no fuckin' law—if he was the law, nine times out of ten he'd asked me for some I.D.—well, I'd a put the pressure on him if Charlie hadn't been with me—we only had about ten minutes until that local pulled out of thar . . .''

The sun had reached the bottom of the ravine and we'd fallen into a long silence. With little ceremony we left the tramps and climbed back into the yard.

8

The yards were gritty and hot and the morning's jungle fires had died out. We left for a few hours to seek shade and coolness along the overgrown banks of the Wenatchee River. The tramp stole a shirtful of apples from a small orchard along the road and they were as cool and uplifting as were the breezes from the river.

A more solid feeling seemed to be forming between the tramp and me. The chemistry of our relationship was affected by our arrival in Wenatchee and the promise of work one short ride up the river. But our feelings toward each other had deepened as well. Carl had taken the role of my teacher and he'd begun to work at making me understand how his life fit together. He became less guarded and revealed more. In doing so, he seemed to have let himself in for a kind of human involvement which is unusual on the road.

But I had, as well, begun to put my cards on the table. I told the tramp of my ambitions as a writer and a photographer and more of what my life was like off the road. Writing was an easy topic to approach because Carl thought writers were able to live a tramp life, which meant he thought they were all like George Bernard Shaw. The photography, however, was more difficult to justify or explain. People

61

will reveal themselves in words but shrink from the camera. The camera was the most untramplike object I could have carried unless, perhaps, I'd taken a portable typewriter along. Yet I wanted photographs of what I was experiencing; in fact I felt a compulsion to record my experiences after three years of preliminary photographic work. I'd taken some photographs earlier on our trip and the tramp hadn't seemed to mind as long as no one else was around. But when we talked about our trip up the river he said: "If you pull that thing out in a car full of men, don't expect *me* to take care of it," which I saw as both a warning to protect my camera and an admonition not to carry on in a way that would make a fool out of him. It was simply that our relationship carried certain unspoken responsibilities. When the tramp buddied up with me he carried me as a badge, part of his identity. It had been clear that morning and I had not, although I'd wanted to, made any photographs of Boston Blackie, or the other tramps we'd jungled with. It had come to the point of deciding whether to remain an outsider in order to bring back photographic documents of how others lived (although there would be no buddying up with Carl or anybody else if that were the case), or to enter the life as fully as I would be able. My friendship with Carl put me past the point of decision; the camera was packed away and rarely emerged again.

We had long, easy conversations in the shade by the river. The tramp began telling me we were heading toward the best tramp job in the country. We'd be in control, he stressed; we'd set out hours and work to our own pace, and we'd work without a foreman looking over our shoulders. And we'd make good money and be able to cook up properly in a cabin. When I didn't comment he said:

"You don't know what it's like for most—usually the contractor gets a job from a farmer, then he goes and hires his help down on skid row. He'll entice them with a bottle of wine. He pays them cheap and he gets top price for the work. That's the way it is in California—even in Oregon—hell, you work for two weeks and owe the man money, just for your canteen check!

"Them guys get up at three o'clock in the morning, ride buses till daylight—work all day and get paid three and a half dollars! And that's stoop labor! Beans, hazel nuts—bending over all day, you wouldn't believe how sore you get!"

"I was in Seattle three years ago," I interrupted, "and they were combing the missions—the "Bread of Life," the "Jericho Mission Inn,"—all those places, for men to pick strawberries—"

"—And I bet they weren't getting three dollars a day! They put in twelve, fourteen, sixteen hours a day! And they charge you a dollar for a hamburger, thirty cents for a ten-cent bottle of pop—and that hamburger is one of those gray jobs like you get in a fast food joint. Everything is double or triple. And they don't tell you that when they give it to you—no siree—they tell you when they show you your bill! And to top it off they charge you a dollar for the ride to work."

I wondered aloud if there might be some way for the tramp to take more control of these situations. Carl didn't let me finish my sentence.

"The fruit tramp? No, no—they don't stick together. They would never stick together—that's why they're tramps. You'll never see it, not as long as the man on the road is a tramp."

"What about the union they're starting down in California—you know, that Chavez?"

"He's helping the Mexicans—he ain't helping me! He means well but he's stayin' with the underprivileged—the Mexican, and the Indian, and the Negro. And you and me? Who cares! Well, you can get a job with his people but I'll bet you won't last long. People stick with their own. You'd get the dirty end of the stick if you worked with those people and it'd be the very same way in these orchards. You Mexicans would get the worst row to hoe, right away. These foremen got friends that come back for years. They get the best and any newcomer, Mexican or otherwise, gets the worst. Of course, they kick back—they know the job and they still got to give the employment people five dollars for giving it to them."

"But how do you stay in a situation where you get fucked over every time you turn around?"

"*They* get in a rut," Carl replied, "they get so they just can't help it."

"What's the way out of that rut?"

"There's only one way out and you're looking at it. Hit the road! Get away from it! Go where the money is! See, I'm free-hearted. I don't have no attachments, not to men and not to things. When I got something, I'll give it to you. You don't have to steal it—I'll give it to you. Like these guys we came up to this morning? If I'd had something the first thing I'd asked them: 'Well, come on, let's eat. Here's the coffee pot—help yourself! . . . You hungry? Here's something to eat!' See, that's the way I am, I can't see another guy go without. Now, old Boston Blackie, he'll have a packsack full and he'll eat out of yours, and then he'll take off and eat his own. Don't you look surprised, you only seen him one time.

"And that gets known—all over the country. People won't travel with him. He says he won't travel with nobody else—well, it's the other way around! But he's bullshitted himself into believing that. You know—he says that he don't want anybody. But they don't want him, and that's the truth! And that's why he's got to go to the mission in the wintertime. 'Course he's getting old—he can't work like I can . . .

"And part of it is the life he leads—it just ain't healthy! Half the time he don't eat right. You heard what he said—sandwich, and a cup of coffee. That's probably all he ate for twenty-four hours.

"But you know we really ain't doing this right, either. Why, you couldn't pack my gear when I'm traveling proper. My chucksack, packsack, and bedroll? Water jug? You couldn't pack it! You wouldn't know how, in the first place. And it must weigh a hundred-fifty pounds. I carry powdered eggs, that sort of thing, dried stuff, raisins, cornmeal, hotcake flour, beans, meat . . ."

"Meat? But it goes bad!"

"Not if you know what you're doing. You cook it and carry it cooked. It keeps quite a while that way. Or carry salt pork to eat. But usually you can buy as you go—there's stores all over nowadays. And I'll even take you to places where these oldtimers got camps with home-made refrigerators! You were there last night—in Sandpoint. If you'd looked outside the boxcar door you'd a seen the trails goin' down by the river. They live there all winter—they all got shacks built. Just before Troy there's a tunnel and there's a junk heap where that Al lives. Used to be a city dump. He'd go in there and scrap copper, and other metals, and sell them. A lot do that. Up and down the tracks pickin' up copper. Why it's forty cents a pound!

"Some of these guys are railroad pensioners—been on the road all their days. Some got army pensions. Some of them are over sixty-two, it all depends. Some guys got hurt working for the railroad and they got their disability. They get a little pension—it ain't enough to live on in the city but it's enough to live on up and down the road. But you can't waste money like these housewives do—a lot of what they buy is just foolishness! You can pay about the same price for a package of pancake flour and make bread all day long . . . You don't need no oven. I can make bread in any campfire in the world. Just take hotcake flour, add cornmeal, eggs, milk, sugar, a little salt, you got a batter right there. Hell, it'll raise a foot! You put it into any kind of fryin' pan and just cook it. And that's good bread—bread that will stick with you. Not like that *city* bread—why that stuff is all air!

"But they don't make it easy for us in these harvest towns. You go into the stores—they got different prices for you. I got a suit of clothes in that plastic bag that cost me seventeen dollars. Pair of pants and a shirt. Bought them up in Oroville. These boots—I bought them right in town here, and they cost me seventeen dollars, too. You can get them in any other store in a different part of the country for thirteen-fourteen at the most.

"You see, this part of the country is based on us. They know we're going to be here—but just a little while. They make sure we don't stay. They don't like the idea of us livin' like this—so, as soon as that harvest is over and they don't need you—out you better get! If you don't, they take your money and run you out—it's as simple as that. Throw you in jail and clean your pockets, then it's right down to the freight yards and on to a freight. Shipped out by the carload. That's it! So you better git while you got some money left!"

"That's probably got something to do with how easy it is to ride freights out of here," I said.

"Something to do with it? They got to put up with it! It's the only way in for most of these people. See, if the police departments here, or in one of these little towns got too rough on the workers, they'd quit coming! And then them city fathers, the merchants, and the farmers would get on the law and make them stop that. That's what they do! Then, when the work is over, they don't give a shit. They don't want you around—they know you'll come back next year. So when the seasonal job is open, they say, 'Well, leave them alone—I need 'em.' Then, when it's over—out we go!

"That's right, it's one needing another. I need them, but they need me more. And that's why I don't work too long for them. They start giving me that gaff—I quit right there. I won't take it; I never take it. Like this eighty-nine and a half hours—well, it was ninety-one and a half hours. But he says: 'Nooo, I'm goin' to dock you this time because that's when you was eatin'.' He docked me a half hour for each meal we ate. The railroad's payin' for my time from the time I left till the time I got back to town—plus meals—but he's putting that extra time in his pocket, see. And I couldn't do nothin' about it. He's makin' thousands of dollars—I'm makin' a few hundred, and he's still got to steal from me! But, if I took a flashlight, or even a pair of gloves—he'd charge me for that. And, if I'd steal it—oh boy! I'm a no-good sonofabitch. But he can steal time from me. That's all right for him to do. And if I say anything about it, well, I ain't got a job in the morning.

"That's why a lot of these guys get disgusted and won't work no more. They either eat on those foodstamps, or go junkin'. Something like that where they're free from that bullshit!"

"Well, most work is like that, in one form or another."

"You got to kiss ass! If it ain't the foreman, it's the owner. It wouldn't be so bad, if they didn't think they were God."

Questions of how the life was lived were, to me, a prelude for the question which I saw as more basic—the issue of what had put them on the road and what sustained them in the life. It is a deceptively simple question for anyone not a tramp, yet the tramps recoil from it. I see it now as part of a larger question concerning why any of us do anything in particular, or why we think we do. Some are quick to point to the influence of either social factors or personality traits, but I think the forces are more subtle and perhaps largely unknowable. Maybe the tramps understand that in part; living in a way that stirs others' interest is of no particular concern to them, and their unwillingness or inability to explain their lives in neat formulas should not be taken as evidence for lack of self-awareness. The tramp lives more in the present, and the dialogue between the issues of what put him there or where he is going next is not very important—even if there were definite answers.

Nonetheless, I told the tramp of my question. At first he did not have much to say. He listed some obvious reasons: troubles with women, or money, or traumatic experiences like the loss of one's family in an automobile accident. Hitting the road, he said, reflected different people's breaking points; some never reached it and others reached it all the time. I pushed the point further and then said: "People here don't talk much about their pasts, do they?" and he shot back: "They don't talk at all about it."

He changed the topic and told me of his plans for settling down. His comments caught me off guard and he said: "Well, I don't mean settle down on some *skid*-row. You got to go to a place where you can do it right. If a guy had a car, and could get in a good locality, he could buy himself a cabin. A place where you could come and go as you want. No regimentation—be on your own! Have a radio or a TV or whatever you want. Go out to these lakes—go fishin', go swimmin'. Live the *good* life. You can still do it!"

"But wouldn't you still get hung up with your drinking?" I asked.

"No, no—you get away from that! Get away from the people that drink. You can work with them—so many hours a day—but then you leave so they can't fuck you up."

I asked him if he knew of any who lived like he described.

"A few of them do," he said, "but the rest—like that old man George—they want to but they can't. Oh, they ride a division and back—they do that until they die. But you know, they outlive a lot of other people. They're healthier. Maybe it doesn't seem like it, but it is a healthier life."

He paused, then he added: "You want to know the reason we're on the road? It's not so different than anybody else. Same reason you see all the cars—all the campers, all along the road. It's wanderlust; it's part of America. In some countries they never get out of the town they were born in! It's the same with the farmers—they never get away; they never get on the road. They got cows to milk and they got to stay."

"But you came from a farm, how did you get started?"

"Well, something like the army comes along. Before the army I had never got out of the country. I don't know what I wanted, probably wanted to be a farmer—that's all I knew. But then I got out in the world and I forgot farming right quick. You never have any money on

67

a farm, you know . . . When I went in the service they were paying twenty-one dollars a month. Shit, that was big money to me . . . just a boy of nineteen . . ."

"But most get out of the army and settle down. What's different about those that don't?"

"Some settle down," he said, "but they didn't stay in long enough. And they probably didn't get transferred all over, like I did. The army's a way of life—you got to drink, or you go nuts. Too much regimentation.

"After the army I started workin' for my brother. Junk business. Learned how to ride freights working for the railroad. Back then it was just a good way of getting from point to point. I guess it hasn't changed much since I began in the early fifties . . . same thing really."

I asked him if there was a point in the beginning of his tramping when he realized he was not going to settle down.

"Army taught me that," he said. "You turn into a tramp in the army. You go where they send you. You lose your home . . . after a while you don't have no home no more. Wherever you stop seems the same after a while. Then when you get out you start living differently. You learn to live out of a pack—pretty soon your bedroll's your home. Do you know that if they catch you with another man's bedroll in Montana you'll go to the penitentiary?" When I looked surprised he said: "Why, when they steal your bedroll they steal your home! That's what I told you!

"Now you hear these guys talk about going back to nature. Well, that's what it is! These guys on the road have been doin' it for years! And now they write books about it! Goin' up north, livin' in the wilderness and all that malarkey—why, that's ancient history to us!

"And these people that go to the communes? They don't last! People can't get along together and they're too soft to work at really livin' in the woods. The only ones that have done it proper are the religious sects and they was born and raised on it. But now even those young people want out of it."

The river was rising and our path was almost under water. We started back toward the jungle, along a soggy path, back up the dusty road and over a small embankment into the yards. We walked to some boxcars abandoned on a siding to rest in the shade.

9

An old tramp, carrying his gear in a gunny sack, limped toward us and announced his presence with a flourish of speedy words: "They call me One-eyed Jack. Call me Jack, or One-Eye. Lost the other when some goddamned kid threw a rock down into the gondola I was riding. That was years ago, and in the meantime I got it frostbit and messed up some more." He said he'd like to "help himself to some of our shade, neighbors," and without waiting for an answer dropped his gear to the ground.

He was tall—over six-foot-three—and wore, as most tramps did, a worn work uniform and leather lace boots, and a long-billed hat. His distinguishing feature was a glazed eye and a deep scar across his forehead, eye and cheek. One whole side of his face seemed to sag and the bad eye was closed. To emphasize a point, he would cock his head and pull open his bad eye, as if to peer intently toward the listener. It was startling to meet the gaze and find yourself staring into the bluish-grey film that covered the eye. But the tramp was talkative and friendly despite his somewhat ferocious appearance, and as Carl was about to hike into town to buy some more beans, I welcomed his company.

Carl was talking about the living arrangements in the cabins, and Jack said: "I ain't about to move into no goddamned cabin with somebody. I don't know anybody that would live with me. I don't give a fuck what you eat—I know what I'm going to eat and if I want a steak I ain't goin' to share it with you. Fuck it! I don't care if you're one man or ten men!

"Shame on me!" he continued. "If you can't afford you're own eats, I don't think I should cut my fuckin' meat down the middle with you."

Carl was quick to agree, but added: "Well, some of those guys won't buy nothing for themselves, either."

"They give the bartender all he wants," Jack answered. "They say: 'How can you afford it?' Fuck, that food costs me good money, and it's going to cost me damn good money this year. Last three times I bought meat I spent close to three and a half, four dollars just to get the goddamned thing. Then I got to take it to the jungle and fuck with it for another goddamn hour. So you're talking about five dollars for a cut of meat. And I'm going to split it with some tramp who won't pull his own weight?"

"Up in Oroville—the last place I worked," Carl said, "a guy named Haskel had one-man cabins. They'd ask you if you'll live with another man. You tell 'em no, an' that's that."

"*Hell* no," Jack added.

"The way I understand it," Carl said, "there ain't too many men up there yet."

"You can't go by word of mouth," One-Eyed Jack answered, "you got some guys'll go up and stay two, three days and be right back. Up and back—back and forth. Can't stay put—and they're lookin' for that job to start."

"So they haven't started up there yet?" Carl asked.

"They're there," Jack stuttered, sounding a little confused. "But you wait a minute. I ain't goin' to tell you they started work up there. Why I'd be a lyin' pigfucker if I told you that! And I'll be god-damned if I'll tell you something I don't know myself! I don't believe in that old garbage! Just because you hear a goddamned rumor . . . why, it don't mean a thing! Now there's probably going to be a few started up there but it may not be the farmers that will hire you and me."

"So it is still a bit early?" I asked.

"Why sure, it's early. Friend, I tell you—last year, or hell, I go back the last twenty years, I'll say ninety percent of them don't start before the eighteenth up to the twentieth, maybe even the twenty-first."

The news took away my spirit like a hot wind through the door of a metal-walled boxcar. Once again I was made aware of how poorly I was able to live the pace of the life. Our money was nearly finished and I was ready to get on with this harvest, but as usual the tramps accepted the news and accommodated themselves to it. They realized their time was cheap and they knew how to survive—and there was nothing they could do about it anyway.

But Carl sensed my disappointment and said: "We can get something. You might not like what you get when you start, but you can always work a few days and get some grub money in your pocket—then leave 'em for something better."

"You know I get a bear in the ass," Jack said, "and he's headed north and I'm goin' south. So I'm going to try to ride him. Hope I can get out to work before Saturday . . . I won't do myself any good before Thursday—because Thursday's the thirteenth and I don't like that day. But fuck that old thirteenth! I'm still going to be in a certain town, tryin' to get out to a certain cabin . . .

"And some of them will let you do a little summer cleaning up so you can make your grub money until you do start. Or you can drive a tractor and do some mowin'. Maybe scatter a few bins for him. But you got to go after it. You got to go up there and face them, that's all."

Jack asked Carl where he was out of and when he told him he'd come from Minneapolis the tramp said: "Where were you floppin', Shorty, over on the island?"

"Who me?" Carl said sharply. "I had my own room!"

"No, what I mean is, were you across the river in Minneapolis on what we call the island?"

"Nicollet Island's all tore down," Carl said. "There ain't hardly a building standing on it. They got new bridges in there now. Almost finished with the second new bridge by now."

"Then where the fuck are the tramps hangin' out?" One-Eyed Jack peered at him.

"You know where the market is, up by the Great Northern depot? That's where I was livin'. The tramps are uptown, and then there's a few of them past that—you know—LaSalle High School."

"At least over on that island you could get a room for fifteen dollars a week, payin' by the week," Jack said, and Carl answered, "No, no, not any more—the winos are up on the north side, up near the Mayflower Hotel—there ain't no cheap hotels left! Them 'cheap hotels' are up to seventy-five dollars a month now!"

"Well," Jack stuttered, "I ain't got no intention of goin' back there. Fuck you people. You can keep your fuckin' Minnesota. I'll be as good to them as they are to me and they aren't sending me no telegram or postcard invitin' me out!"

"You carry a lot of stuff with you," I said after the tramp had become silent.

71

"I'm goin' to tell you a little story, friend," the tramp peered toward me with his sightless eye. "I got enough stuff for two men, but I got some winter stuff I'm not goin' to throw away. I'll be goddamned if in another month if I'm going to be payin' four dollars a piece for those insulated underwear and then only wear them two or three times, or maybe six or seven, then throw them away. Four dollars is four dollars to me. Same thing about them drawers. Guys say, 'Well, that's too warm clothes for this here weather' . . . Well, here we go again! That's whatever a man wants to wear! I have to live with these legs. An' whatever a man lives with, well, that's his business.

"Last winter I went to Wyoming to herd sheep and I needed 'em and I didn't have 'em. Twenty-eight below . . . sittin' on a horse. Oh, that sheepherding's got its good and bad points—you got a dog to bring 'em back and to head 'em up, that stuff. You got to get out about seven-thirty, quarter-to-eight in the morning, and you got to bring them in at dark. And them damn things don't like to eat. You can take them out—just about a quarter-to-seven, about the break of day in the winter—and they won't eat anything because they don't want to tuck their heads down into that cold snow, and pull that grass out of that fuckin' snow . . . an' I don't blame 'em! They want to wait till it warms up! Then they run like a bunch of goddamned antelope. Some days I would make three miles each way—well, buddy, that's six bucks a mile. But that's a goddamned cold mile, every one of them!

"And then that jackass camp man had to bring an old fuckin' mare and her colt out there—that really tore me up. I was only out there for a month and a half—I left that job the fifteenth of February. I'd stayed longer but that fuckin' colt would get right up from under me—kicked the shit right out of me! You know what would have happened if I'd a had a twenty-two?"

"You'd a shot the camp man for bringin' it out there," Carl laughed.

"That's a dirty Irish trick," Jack continued. "They got twenty-some horses but instead they put that goddamned thing off on me. I landed on my ass three times—she was a bad sonofabitch. And she'd run off and leave you there! She'd already run off and left three before I came on the job—twenty-five miles up to fifty miles from no place, yeah, you had to watch her all the time. I always kept a rope, thick as my finger, on her halter."

Jack was really the first tramp we'd talked to who'd had a lot of

72

seasons in the orchards. I was interested in how many apples he really expected to be able to pick. He said: "Oh, I usually run four . . . It all depends on how many fuckin' brush piles I have to chop out. If I'd run over twelve bins I wouldn't know it; I just stay with it till I'm done for the day—I don't pay no heed to how many I think I'm goin' to get. Some days you just can't work like you think you can."

"They payin' six this year?" Carl asked.

"I don't know about it," Jack answered, "they might be payin' six for the goldens; five and a half for the reds."

"A guy should be able to make twenty a day here," Carl said.

"I figure, if I get in young trees," Jack said, "an' I can work off a ten-footer—there will be days I'll go out there and get five bins, or even six bins. But I want you to hear me loud and clear—I'm goin' to high-roll to do it. I ain't goin' to tell no-one that, but that's how it's going to be."

"I don't know how many I can pick," Carl said, "I've never done it before. I might be no good at all!"

"You got to high-roll to get those good days," Jack said, "you got to know how to set your ladder—take about three or four sets to a tree and run up and down that ladder like a fuckin' monkey! *That's* high-rolling.

"But they won't pay you off out there—the insurance won't pay you a cent if you fall off the top of a twelve-footer. You got to keep off that last step! Use that last step for just a minute, well, partner, don't you go telling anybody about it! And don't you go standing on the top of that ladder and reaching over the back of your head. Reset your ladder and do it right!"

"I won't go past the last two steps," Carl said. "I brace myself against the ladder with my knee. No, that's prunin', it might be different pickin'."

"It won't be every day I'll get five or six bins," Jack said, " 'cause I won't have that kind of steam."

"Some of them make good money," Carl said, " 'course they got great big hands—they pick three or four apples at a time."

"If I have to fuck with them goldens," Jack answered, "I'll make the farmer furnish me with gloves. 'Cause if you leave finger marks, well, it's 'Goodbye partner!' If he ain't got any gloves, I tell him to go and get some—it's his goddamned apples I'm trying to pick. I can get twice as many reds as I can goldens. Most of the time when I come out of them fuckin' reds I got two or three apples—that's part of high-rollin'. An' if they're in clusters, I'll go up on them like that there" (motioning with both hands) "and I don't lose any of them. When I come out of that cluster I come out with all them fuckin' things, and I don't bruise any of them. You can't separate them. You start that shit you're goin' to knock the others down. You try to take one off, the other sonofabitches will drop. You try to take three off and the other two will drop . . ."

"Take 'em all!" Carl interrupted.

"What you got to do," Jack stammered, "is get your hands underneath there, like, and come off there with the whole bundle. You might drop one—but one ain't like three or four. But if they hit the ground—you better leave them there, 'cause if you put 'em in the bin an' they catch you, well, it's 'Goodbye, brother!' for that, too. You got to leave them when they hit that ground—even when they fall in that deep grass."

After a pause, Jack continued: "But you know it's not always you can get a train up there. There might be an up-on-top ride, or you might have a loaded gondola, but I've watched one after another pull out of here with nothing but sealed reefers. Last time I went up I hitch-hiked—didn't have no trouble, guy took me right up there with him. He was shit-faced drunk. Yeah, I thumbed this asshole—he was going to Omak—that's where they got their employment office. I was headed in there between Omak and Okanogan to get some of those old foodstamps. He stops and says: 'You headed to Okanogan?' I says: 'Yeah, I'm goin' over there to get some foodstamps.' 'By the way,' he says, 'you ain't lookin' for a job thinnin', are you?' I says, 'You're damn right I'm lookin' for a job thinnin'—now, wait just a minute—that's *if* there's enough money in it!'—'Well,' he says, 'I'm payin' two and a quarter.' So I told him to just turn it around, but first he had to take me over to the Great Northern depot—I left my gear over there in the weeds. And I got started about twenty after eight and they stop—this is the damnedest outfit I ever seen!—they only work eight hours a day! They quit about two-thirty, quarter-to-three, three o'clock . . . When I got out to the place, I got myself into a cabin and the old boy says, 'Do you want to work this mornin'? 'Why,' I says, 'you damn right I want to work this mornin'! I didn't come out here for a vacation, friend, I came out here to work!' Sure, I would have liked to lay in, who the hell wouldn't? I always like to lay in a half day to see where in the fuck I am. So I am going to start workin' and I asked what time is it? He answers that it is twenty after eight; we'll start today at eight. He gave me that time extra! But then I told him that tomorrow afternoon if he was fixin' to go into town I'd like to go along and get some groceries; I figured I could eat apples for a day and then draw the second. But he made it loud and clear: he'd take me in town but from then on I'd have to get my own way. And I thought, why you sonofabitch! You got me over the hoopy-hoopy now! But I was going to make the week anyway, 'cause I got a little bill down the line here, and I want to get that bill straightened around. I could send him the money, but I don't like this money-order business, I'd rather go back and pay the man, lookin' him in the eye, and know fuckin' well he got it! Then he can't say: 'Somebody got to it, I never seen it,' or some other old bunch of horseshit. So I made it four days and seven hours—that was with that short day. Then on Saturday I quit. They were only going to work a half a day anyhow. An' I thought: What the fuckin' hell is this, anyway! Now, some of these guys and most farmers know this—on Sundays they only want to go out and work long enough to get two bins, or three bins—then the rest of the day they spend sitting around washing their clothes. Well, I'm going to tell you something: anytime I go work for that farmer, Sunday's the same as Monday to this boy. Because look—by the tenth of October, or the fifteenth at the very most—she's all over with. And then I got all kinds of time to wash my clothes! Or in the evening, when I leave that brush pile, I get myself a bucket, dig out a couple of old fuckin' shirts, and you probably know, Shorty, that it's hot enough in that cabin over night to get that shirt three-quarters dry. More than three-quarters sometimes. And I can put on a damp shirt any day—that Sunday is the same as Monday to me. How does that old song go?" He knotted his forehead and recited: "That– belly– has– to– be– fed– just– the– same– on– Sunday– as–it– does–on–Monday."

Carl chuckled but remained silent. The old tramp got a second or third wind and said: "Well, I'll tell you one thing, neighbor, and now I don't like to be tellin' a man how to live his life, but you still got to be careful on that ride up the branch. You got some phony bastards, and they run in packs. Indians. And there's some white sons-of-bitches just as bad as that Indian. Our own color!"

"They'll jump you in a minute," Carl agreed, "only this kid don't ever listen to me!" His voice softened and he added: "Course you might get lucky and get a bunch of good guys in a car."

Jack spoke: "Well, I pulled one here a couple of years ago, and it griped me from my asshole to my toes. I don't usually pull that stunt, riding with a whole bunch of Negroes and I been on the road for thirty years. I never did it before, but I did it that time. I just don't want to fuck around with that colored guy—I just don't want that sonofabitch in there. But this time I got in up there in town and then of course there's a couple of smart white sons-of-bitches that got in that boxcar with a half gallon of that old fucked-up wine. They was trying to get them boys to drink that wine so they could fuck with them—you know—jackroll them. And one of them white boys got a little sour, because people weren't taking that bottle. So one of the Negroes straightened him right out. He says: 'Fellas, everybody was happy till you two guys got in here with that goddamned stuff.' He says: 'I'm not drinkin'—and some of my friends are not drinkin'. So I think that you better leave them alone.' And them two got a-hold of their hats, and said 'So long, partner,' 'cause there were five or six of them sons-of-bitches in there!"

"You get a good one, or a bunch of them good ones—they're all right," Carl said.

"I rode all the way to where I was goin'," Jack continued, "and not once—hear me loud and clear—not even one bummed me for a match! Now if I'd a been in there with a bunch of white guys—there ain't no tellin' how many matches or how many cigarettes I'd've had to hand over."

The bull local was almost completely made up. I wanted to find a place to ride, but Carl told me to relax—the crummy was down at the other end of the yard and the brakelines still hung unattached. He decided that we needed food after all and took some of my change to get some more bread and beans.

One-Eyed Jack stayed behind to talk, even though he'd lost half his audience. He looked me over—I had the feeling that he hadn't paid much attention to me—and he said: "If I didn't have to work to live, work to buy my clothes and my grub, then *damn* that work! Do you know what I mean? Fuck that work! I can get along without it! But partner, I ain't going to sell myself short—I can go to any of those orchards and find a job. They know me—I work hard for them. And I usually keep my hair cut pretty short, but now I'm short—I only got a few pennies to buy beans till I get something going. But you understand me, loud and clear, I'll get up here and get a few weeks work in, and if we happen to have one wet morning, you know, if it rains at night and we can't get our work in, then I'll go to town and get all this brush pile knocked off.

"It was the last of July when I got my last hair cut," he said, "and if I'd've used my head I could have got one before now. But I decided I wanted to stretch. But I don't blame you for it, I blame my own ignorance. That's it. I seen a fella yesterday, hell, he was on the job five weeks, and when he got through with his trip to the tavern he didn't have nothin' but a few cents change in his pockets. You might have seen him in the yards. He had a little yeller cap on. Big red-faced guy and a little-bitty yeller fucked-up cap. He and I jungled together back in Spokane for a while. I didn't ask him to get off that train up here, I figure that's something a man has got to work out for himself! But he jumped and we was heading down to this jungle I know and he says, 'It's too far to walk.' Well, shit, there ain't nobody goin' to tell me what to do or where to get off—so I went down and jungled by myself. So I don't share my beans this time. And with what I got in that jar I can make three days. It might be a slim get-by, but I can do it. But how are you going to get by these days? Potatoes, *potatoes* are twenty-some cents a pound. What a bunch of bullshit! I can eat that old macaroni. Macaroni ain't no cheaper, but I can get two meals out of a pound. I can't do that with potatoes. When I start eatin' a pound of potatoes I just got to finish! Restaurants the same. Goin' out of sight. I know damn well you know what I'm talking about when I say *spare* ribs. You get a little salad, a few french fries, and your spare ribs. Two dollars and a half. If you want to call that a cheap meal—well, I don't see nothin' cheap about a bunch of old bones—very little meat on those spare ribs, any fool knows that! Two and a half for a meal? Why, suck my butt! If I was a millionaire I wouldn't buy that kind of junk! I'd put in another half buck, or six bits, and buy myself a roast beef dinner. It's two and a half, I'd put another dollar on it and make it three and a half and help myself to some good meat!" He paused, and then said reflectively: "When I'm workin' it strikes me different. If I'm workin'—*fuck* the goddamned money. I'm going to buy the food! I'll walk in that store and see a piece of meat—if it costs two dollars and six bits to keep my gut full, that's part of my livin'. I'm only on this world for a short time, and I'm damn sure if I got this money in my pocket—if I'm workin'—I'll eat. Now I can get along on this other kind of grub—this old hard grub when I'm not workin'. Like I'm eating today. Macaroni and beans, shit like that. And I'll eat a little of that, too, when I get myself situated. But I won't eat too much of it once I get going. Now, some of these people start whinin': 'Oh, I'll wait till I get . . .'—I say, *damn* down the road. Damn down the road. Shit, *fuck* that down the road! You're liable to go to a bank, get that sonofabitch cashed and somebody's liable to waylay you— knock you on the head before you even get on the train! Lose every dime. And there's no lookin' back then, at all the good eatin' you did off that money. So I ain't goin' to wait till I get on the road. I'm goin' to eat that sonofabitch up—part of it, anyway—while I'm workin' . . .

"And I won't buy eggs, and I used to eat the hell out of them. You know where a chicken scratches on a farm? I like that kind of egg. But the co-op eggs? No, no, no. I wouldn't take it if you were giving it away! I was up there in Montana and the old man was goin' up town to buy some groceries, to cook up for the hired hands. I told him I didn't like those eggs. No, I'll tell you, I really don't like those eggs! I think I was on that job two days after that; I just said, 'I'll be seeing you.' I didn't try to insult him, I just walked down the road. See, a lot of people take advantage of us tramps. I don't believe in that. So when the man starts to push a little, I just say, 'So long, partner.' And that's that.

"I can almost taste that fucked-up feed them chickens ate to make that egg. Some kind of chemical. They keep feeding 'em and they don't let 'em sleep. They give them chemicals to make 'em grow fast—why, it's no wonder those eggs taste like that! Now, I don't know how you're going to take what I'm about to say—but I think, neighbor, that these chemicals they're putting in our meat and produce—I think that's why so many people get so many cancers and so many heart attacks. I'm old-fashioned, and I only got a third grade education, but I really believe that! I'll go back before your time— thirty years ago you didn't have very many goddamned people with these heart attacks and this other bullshit! It's the life, too—new car, new home, fancy wife. And they're payin' for it—they got to high-roll—they can't say no. That may be the way *you* want to live, but friend, it ain't for me. I figured that one out long time ago . . ."

Jack wandered off a few minutes later to find his ride up the branch. I didn't have enough to say to hold his interest and that was disappointing. It wasn't really that I didn't have much to say but more that I was not practiced in the style of tramp oration, in which the stories are taken up by others and the banter goes round and round. It involves a degree of acceptance; an equality based on shared experience. Carl had taken the back seat to Jack but he'd encouraged him with a quip, a chuckle, or even a raised eyebrow. As much as I'd been on the road I wasn't seasoned enough to be on even roughly equal footing with One-Eyed Jack, and as soon as the exchange became one-sided it ended—the tramp packed up his stories and hiked away.

10

The ride up the branch! But what, indeed, was the branch—rail, river, or water? The river and the rail line wound north together, but it was the irrigated river water that made the valley a green band among brown hills. The rails brought empty refrigerator cars in the late summer and, of course, the workers. Short weeks later the reefers would carry away the crop, and somewhere in the nooks and crannies of the train the tramps would ride out as well. The only irony may have been that it all took place so easily, so neatly. The crops grew; the workers circulated in and circulated out with the fruit, and most of the money generated in the process never left the county.

All of my freight riding had been in the summers and on main lines through largely deserted freight yards so I was unprepared for the Wenatchee yard suddenly come alive with men carrying packs and bedrolls, all looking for a ride to a job. Usually a tramp can pick and choose his company and he usually rides alone, even if it means missing a train. But there was an urgency among the men in the Wenatchee yard to get out, to get north, so when Carl and I crowded into one of the two empties on the train, we packed in shoulder to shoulder with twenty-five or thirty more.

Our new identity as workers was made apparent when the engineer of the train stopped by to talk with the carload of tramps. The engineer is the man to whom all pay deference; the train stops so he has only a short walk to the engine and he does not stop to pass the time of day with brakemen or car knockers as he walks, in his clean coveralls, directly to the cab of the diesel engine. But that day the engineer ambled over, leaned in our car and told us politely that he was going to whistle-stop in Pateros so if any of us wanted off there we'd have to jump on the run. He said he'd give two whistles just before he slowed as a warning, then wished us a good trip before walking on. No one but me seemed surprised by the exchange.

The atmosphere in the car was one of guarded suspicion. There was none of the banter that rounds the jungle fires; none of the easy camaraderie I'd come to expect even among strangers in a car. I saw One-Eyed Jack, but when our eyes met there was no sign of recognition, or greeting. He sat, as did the others, watching silently and holding onto his gear.

The riders had separated into two groups—some at the head of the car stood around a couple gallons of Thunderbird wine and drank in long gulps. As they became drunk they caroused near the door and offered their wine to the others, one after another. Nearly all turned them down but some were torn between their images and the cool drink of sweet wine. When the tramps we'd talked with in the gully joined the drinkers, Carl spat, under his breath, "Riffraff!"

Most of the men with the wine carried no gear and wore mismatched and ill-fitting clothes. We were all dirty but they were filthy with matted hair and their own body dirt. I watched one in particular who was gesturing and jabbering when Carl interrupted my thoughts, speaking in a low voice: "That one you're looking at—well, that's a jackroller looking around for some to roll. He ain't drunk—he's just pretendin' to be. He won't mess around now—too many people, but you wait, he'll be around. Maybe on a train, maybe in a town. We'll see him again."

The train pulled out smoothly and we were soon traveling along a beautiful river bank. The tracks were halfway up bare brown hills on the west bank of the river, so like the night before the long rays of the sun lit the train intermittently with long slanting rays. For a few moments the sun shone through the doors of the car and the shadows of the tramps stood out like black giants on the opposite bank of the narrow river. The drinkers became quiet and moved to the front of the car, and others took their places sitting crosslegged before the doors staring as if transfixed by the landscape and the river that spun by below.

Within an hour we reached our destination. Carl coached me on the fine points of jumping on the run; crouch over and swing forward so to land running; try to stay on your feet but roll if you have to, swing away from the train by pushing off from a lever at the rear edge of the door.

As the train slowed, ten tramps lined up behind the door like paratroopers. An old man in a green work uniform and a red-billed baseball hat stood by the front of the door, complaining that there was no room for him in the line. The train seemed to be moving quite fast when the engineer sounded the whistle. Carl threw our gear through the door and the line of tramps swung off the train. The old man went out near the front of the door and landed badly. My turn came and I swung into a running leap five feet to the slanting trackbed of sharp rocks. I lost my balance and went sprawling but Carl stayed on his feet and as the train gained speed I watched similar scenes along the track—men leaping, some gracefully and others with clumsy abandon, from the cars onto the rocks. Some fell and others rolled, but they all looked as if they'd done it a hundred times before.

The men picked themselves up, dusted off and collected their gear. Some headed toward town, Carl said to get drunk, and the oldtimers held back, forming small groups. The old man got up slowly and was limping. Another tramp, clean in workclothes and carrying an airline bag and a bedroll tied with rope, approached the old man and said: "Ya okay, oldtimer?" A few words were exchanged before the old man hobbled off by himself, weighed down by his gunny sacks of gear.

We picked up our gear and then Carl pointed to some bushes at the base of the hills: "Over there," he pointed, "that's where the jungle is. We'll wait a few minutes until this place clears out and then we'll go over there and eat."

We milled around until the tramps seemed to melt into the countryside. I was sitting on the ground resting against my pack and chewing on a weed watching the sky darken when Carl finally motioned that it was time to go. We found the jungle and Carl left immediately for wood, while I stayed with the gear and looked for a can to heat water in.

Carl returned with dried brush and heavy sticks. The fire was quickly underway and water heated in a coffee can Carl had found up the hill. We opened a can of beans and I groaned and complained and Carl humored me, promising that when we started working he'd buy me a can of Jack Mackerel that I could eat all by myself. While the water heated I looked through my pack to check my camera and found two carrots. Carl eyed the camera and I asked him again what he thought of the idea of dragging a camera along on a trip such as ours.

"Heavy as hell, I'd imagine," he replied, then added, "I've seen other people do that. They come down in the streets, though. But the first thing they'll ask you is, 'Hey, will you tell me something, if I buy you a bottle?' Or, 'Can I take your picture for a drink.' For a lousy quarter. And you ask them why, and it's 'Oh, we're just . . .' You know, they give you a phony excuse . . . I just walk away.

"Some guys will try to act a part they're not, you know. They're phony. You can spot them right away if you got any intelligence at all."

"I don't try to make out any different than what I am," I said, "I told you what I was doing."

"I ain't talkin' about you. Anyway I already told you what I thought of your camera.

"You know," he changed the subject, "most of your casual labor offices are on the skid row. So if you work any kind of casual labor and you want to make a fast buck that's where you'll go. It's where you can make it when you're flat broke."

The tramp picked up a carrot and eyed it thoughtfully: "Well, I suppose you're going to be tellin' me to eat this fuckin' carrot," he said. "Hell, starting this time of night it'll be ten o'clock before I get it ate!"

We watched a tramp walking alone along the tracks toward the orchards. "That's that old guy," Carl said, "lookin' for a place far away from everybody else . . . He'd better, he's getting too old to be makin' it on the road. Did you see him come out of that boxcar? I thought he wasn't going to get up!" Then he added when I didn't answer: "We got to be careful, too. We don't want nobody stumbling up on us. If you get hit over the head with one of those short-handled props you'll never know what happened."

But my thoughts were on the lonely looking figure limping along the tracks. "How old is he, Carl?" I asked.

"Sixty, I'd say. Too old. It gets rough when you get old. People start takin' advantage." After a few seconds he added: "I don't look my age—that old—when I clean up. My face looks bad, but when I get feeling better and get my uniform on—then I look okay." I didn't know what to say. I thought of the old man and the life seemed desolate in the advancing darkness.

Carl tended the fire and heated water. After a few minutes I said: "All right, I want you to eat this carrot, and I don't want any shit about it."

"No-no-no . . ."

"You get the big one, too."

"No, uh-uh."

"You don't want it? What's the matter with you? You haven't been getting your vegetables! Now Carl, this one here's got your name right on it!"

"*You* eat it—I can't chew the cocksuckers. It would take me hours to chew 'em! Only got that one tooth up there to bite with and haven't got no teeth at all on top on the one side, and on the other I've got four but the one underneath is loose! So I've got one on top with one below to chew on—otherwise I've got to gum it . . . Oh, I used to eat them, I used to pick them out of the fields at home. I like them when they're a little bit smaller than that . . . when they're not quite as big, the heart is the best . . .

"When I was a kid we had to hoe the garden. We'd carry a salt and pepper shaker—you know, one with both mixed in. If we'd get a little hungry or thirsty, we'd pick up a tomato and eat it. We grew them all—carrots, potatoes, chards, onions, beans, spinach. It was a dairy farm—hundred and twenty acres. When I was young, though, they lost it. Late depression years, they lost it for taxes. Then my old man took off on us and left my mother with seven little kids. She worked the farm herself. Hell, when I was ten, eleven years old I worked like a man."

"Is your mother still alive?"

"Yeah, she's alive."

"Do you still see her?"

He answered: "Oh yeah . . . I go there before I get drunk. That's where a lot of my money goes! She's old. She gets old age pension—social security, and that ain't enough . . .

"She married again, and I can't stand the sonofabitch she married. She couldn't get along with one German, she had to marry two!

"Yeah, ours is a mixed-up family," he continued, "I've got a sister who's an ordained minister in South Bend, Indiana. My youngest sister is married to a vice-president in Duluth, Minnesota. Old Roland owns a big junk business in Warsaw and the rest of them—I don't know what they're doing. Billy, I think, works in a factory. Kinda lost track of old Billy . . . Nobody says nuthin' about him . . .

"And that old brother Roland! He's more of a fuckin' Jew than a real one. The town I grew up in is gettin' big now, over fifty thousand. There are all those stores like J. C. Penney's, Woolworths, Kinney's Shoes and all the other shoe stores. He charges them five dollars to pick up their garbage. You know, the trash. He puts the cardboard on the side and he sells that to the Jews! And do you know that pays his expenses. Just what he sells to the Jews! Then what he charges for the stop—and some of this is every *day*—he puts in the bank. Brand new car every year—new trucks every other year. I ask him for a loan and it: 'I'm broke, Carl, can't do it.' I never asked him again.

"I helped him build a fifty-two by thirty ranch-style house for nothin'. All one fuckin' fall and half the winter. Yeah, they expect it when they ask you, but when you ask them it's different."

His voice trailed off. In a few minutes he said: "We ain't in such a bad situation, you know. They want us to be invisible, now, like we don't exist, but it's not completely one way or another. Some of these little towns treat the worker all right—to the merchants we're business—don't you think they see all that green color?

"And if the owners like you they'll ask you to stay around to pick up the props. They might let you hang around in the cabins till prunin' starts, then hire you again.

"And if you get a job with certain people," he continued, "you may only work six days. They may not let you work Saturday because they're Seven Day Adventists . . . generally the people you work for are real nice." I was surprised and Carl repeated: "Real nice, but now some of the people they got workin' for *them*—the police, the fore-

back to the South End; Boston

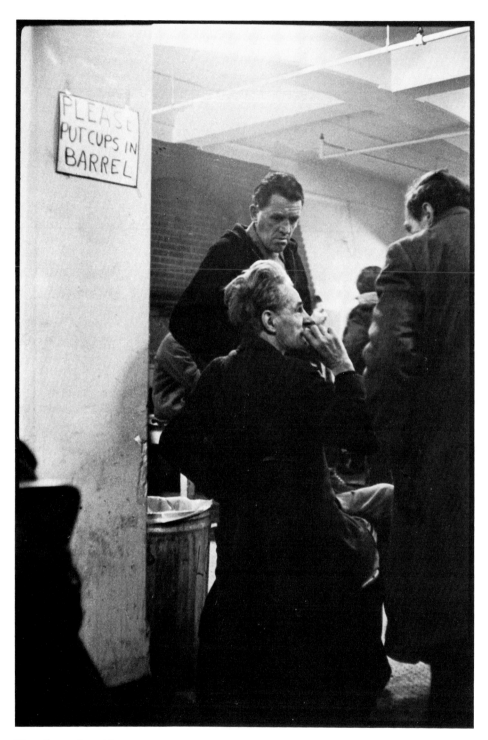

Pine Street Inn; Boston

on the Bowery; New York City

on the Bowery; New York City

Seattle skid row

Boston

Seattle; some small help

Boston

junking; Boston

husband and wife looking for a bootleg bottle six o'clock, Sunday
morning; Boston, winter

junking; Boston

daytime peace; Seattle skid row

bindle stiff off the road; Seattle

mission stiff; Seattle

homeguard; Boston

Boston skid row

man, and some of the merchants—they look down on you. You're dirt. They want your money, but they don't want you. 'Course you can see the hypocrites in some of them owners, too . . .

"But everything changes in these towns when a thousand workers come in. Only a few will be from Brewster, the rest from all over—Spokane, Seattle, Wenatchee. They have ads all over the west in the farm labor offices. This is the Okanogan River valley—the best apple country in the west and we're sitting right in the middle of it.

"So you got to expect your riffraff, too. Some of them—they get money and the first goddamn thing they do is go up to the tavern. They start performin', and cussin', and makin' advances at the women in the streets—there you go! Foul language . . . They don't make themselves welcome!

"But most of them here think: 'Here comes that money!' Most spend all they make right here. They say they get robbed—well, some do—but most of them spend it. They go to jail and the judge takes it. Or the police get to it first.

"You'd be surprised," he continued, "some of these guys are so anxious to get to work. They work two days, three days, maybe a week. Then they're gone. Five or six days later here they come back, and they hire them all back.

I showed my surprise.

"Why, *sure*," he emphasized, "Hell, they have to!

"Now you saw how quick some of those guys took that wine. That's a typical apple picker, that wino. He comes up here and won't work. That one didn't have no clothes—no nuthin.' He's just goin' from town to town bummin'. Probably got his clothes from the Salvation Army, or else he's workin' somewhere around here, out on a drunk and started runnin'. His bottle run out, that's the matter. No more drinkin'. But, you know, some of those winos will get out and work their ass off for that bottle. Make it about three days, and have forty or fifty dollars comin'. Maybe sixty. And then they'll go out and you won't see them until every fuckin' dime of that is gone—damn!"

We spoke a few minutes more while the fire died down and then packed our gear. It was dark and Carl had lost his salt shaker, but he wouldn't think of leaving without it. The moon had risen and it was almost full. We had our gear together but still the tramp did not want to go. "We'll wait," he said, "until everything is quieted down."

I asked him to tell me about sheepherding.

"Nothing to it," he said, "you just go out and watch the sheep. They got a camp man that is supposed to come around once a day and see you. It's a federal law. Yeah," he said, "that's a good life—*clean*. You go to Utah, Wyoming, Montana, Washington, Idaho—they all got sheep. Summer herding up in the mountains pays anywhere from three-fifty to four-fifty a month. Food, usually a house on wheels, a sheepwagon. Some give a horse, some don't. They all furnish a dog. It's a lazy man's life but it gets cold. It's a good place to dry out.

"Sometimes you got to help the ewe give birth. I had to turn a lamb around—then pull him out. Stuck my arms in past my elbows. And he lived. That's when you start earnin' your money. Then you got to learn 'em how to *suck*—you know, suck their mother. They're dumb, dumb animals."

"I thought everything knew how to suck."

"Not your lamb," Carl replied, "you got to teach him. Just show him once and that's it. Just show him once and then he knows. You just have to show him that first time.

"Then when he gets older you got to cut their tails off—if they're a male you castrate 'em. Hell, there's a lot of work to it. And they get a lot of diseases! Gets too cold—they die. Or they pile up and suffocate. You got a whole goddamned herd to take care of and the goddamned things are dumb!

"Those guys that herd are loners—you know, like that One-Eyed Jack—that airdale we talked to," Carl explained. "Do you remember that airdale? That's what they are. See, they don't want nothin' to do with anyone else no more. They get by themselves. I camp-tended for old Louis Josell in Lowela, Oregon, one year. He told me: 'Carl, if you ever get a herder that won't talk to you—and when he sees you coming walks the other way, or tries to hide from you—well, you let me know and I'll get a replacement.' They go a little out of their head. Too much loneliness. They're the kind of guy that'll go out and make, say, three to five thousand dollars and come in and spend it. They stay out that long. When they come in—women, drinkin', or they just give it away. They're just an alcoholic—it's only that they go at it periodically . . . They'll give it to the bartender and he'll steal part of it. And all of his buddies will help him spend it. He'll have lots of buddies!

Everybody will stay drunk until he's broke, then he'll borrow two or three hundred to get back out to work and start all over again.

"They're oldtimers, not exactly tramps," he explained. "They're usually old ranchhands that are too old to do hard work, but your cowboy don't like a sheepherder. Cattlemen don't either—the sheep graze the grass too short. They see a ranger once in a while, or a horseman goin' through the country, but usually it's just that wide open country, just like these hills."

Carl put a few more sticks on the dying fire. "I used to go up to Pasco, Washington, first of February every year. Then I'd work in Montana until freeze-up. That's October in Montana. Work in wheat or on the ranches. Then I'd go home and spend some time there and then go to California and drive truck until the first of February when I'd start all over again. But I gave up that California trip. Now maybe I'll go out to Great Falls and work the ranches. Or back to Minneapolis—plenty of work there come winter time. But lately I've been coming up here—I'm beginning to like the work up here. If you get a good orchard you're set, you can have yourself a good situation. You can get an automobile, and come and go as you want. And this really isn't hard work."

I interrupted: "What would you see for yourself in ten years? If you got what you wanted, that is."

The question was out of sync; inappropriate.

"Christ!" he said, "I don't know! That would be dreaming!"

I asked him, very clumsily: "Do you dream?"

"It don't matter what I want in the next ten years. It's what I get that counts. Your dreams? That's all they are—dreams."

"But what do your dreams consist of?"

"I don't dream no more. Not that way. All I want, like I told you the other day—is to own a piece of ground. It don't have to be too big—just enough to sustain myself so I don't have to work for somebody else. But, ah shit, do you know how much that land costs? Little portion would cost you thousands. I'd be dead before I had that kind of money."

I realize now I was trying to change the tramp in a fundamental way. It was easy to see that the money for the cabin would be no trouble; money came and went like the seasons. It was the connections that ownership of land entailed that the tramp would have no part of, and when I asked the tramp why he didn't put some money away for such a possibility he just yawned and changed the subject.

11

Loud, raucous voices came out of the darkness. Carl motioned me closer. "It's those two we saw this morning. You saw what they were eatin' in the boxcar, didn't you? They were eatin' candy! And those sandwiches came from that shelter, I'm sure of that. They are good today, I saw them heating up a whole pot of butter beans and bacon when I went to get the water. Then they was eatin' ice cream, soda pop, candy. When I came back from the store they asked me if I used foodstamps, and I says, 'No, I use money.' 'God-*darn*,' that big one says, 'why didn't you tell me—I would've given you stamps for that money!' They wanted money and they had foodstamps—that's how they eat that junk because there are only certain foods you can get with the stamps. So they're just wasting their money. Squanderin' it. Even thirty-six dollars worth don't last forever.

"I've had to get those stamps before and we could have stopped on our way here and got them. I know where they're at—I've got them there in Idaho. But there's a difference with those two—they ain't got no pride! I knew I would come out here and go right to work. I'd get something, even if it's loading a boxcar—I've never been that bad where I couldn't find a day's work—enough to keep me going. But to take something like that—those food stamps you get for nothing—most of them lie about it anyhow—you have to lie to get them and then spend it on a candy bar and soda pop and ice cream—why it just ain't right!

"Think of all that money, and the food they wasted today—you can live cheap on this road! There are a lot of tricks you don't know. That guy taught you one today—save your beans, carry a bottle, anything, and take them with you. Rice, beans, carrots, anything. When you get done eatin' and you're not hungry any more, pack 'em up! Take 'em with you! When you ain't hungry you don't think ahead. Up here you

88

pack in a few apples. You saw it—those guys asking me for an apple—why didn't they get some for themselves? They could have got them just as easy as I did! They didn't think ahead enough to have an apple in their pocket riding in a freight along a hundred miles of orchards—no apples, no tobacco, no nothin'. Bummin' a match to light the cigarette they got from their buddy. *Or me.* Did you hear that other guy? He says, 'Roll two while you're at it!' . . . Why, the cheap bastard.

"But you tell me," he said, "what was different about all those guys that were bummin' on the train?"

"No gear?"

"Those bums had low-quarter shoes. Low-quarter shoes with stocking falling over their ankles. Holes in the shoes, holes in the pants. Your tramps, even if they were dirty had working man's clothes—and they wore boots and a hat. Did you see that guy across the car? *That's* your tramp. He don't talk much—he don't speak until he's spoken to. Did you see how he was carryin' his bedroll? Tied like mine. Clean shaved . . . You know, I know him. I might have him confused with somebody else, but I don't think so. I either worked with him, or we crossed paths someplace else. He wouldn't give me no straight answers. He was light but when I says: 'What happened to your packsack,' he didn't say nothin'. He's the kind of man that don't want too much known about him. Either he's got his packsack hid somewhere or he's just up here to 'make a wild' and he don't want to lose it."

"He had a look about him," I said, and Carl interrupted: "He sure didn't have nothin' else! Just that bedroll. 'Course he could have a change of clothes rolled up in there."

The tramps in the darkness began catcalling and yelling; hooting their echoes. Carl said: "That's what I can't stand—that loud talk on somebody else's property—you can hear them all over! And just one call to the cops and they'd take us all in . . .

"That's the kind with no respect, no respect for anything, not even themselves. I heard that guy talking about apples but when the train stopped in Everett, right by an apple tree, he just stood there lookin'! Couldn't be bothered to get themselves an apple—too heavy to carry. They're like all these guys, they don't want them until they're hungry."

He rose and stretched. "Well, I don't know about you, but I'm about ready to turn in." I was about to pour water on the coals of the fire when Carl stopped me: "Are you going to go find more for our coffee tomorrow?" Then he kicked dirt on to the ashes, and picked up the tin can and put it in his pack.

The hills rose steeply behind us and the tracks were perhaps fifty yards in front of the jungle. The orchard lay across the tracks; beyond flowed the Okanogan River. The lights of the town shone in the distance.

We gathered our belongings and walked wordlessly across the tracks, into the most obscure corner of the orchard. An orange moon had risen and lit our way with an eerie yellow light. I followed Carl to an area where the weeds were higher than our knees, then we worked our way under a tree with a canopy of branches. The branches were heavy with fruit and reached to the ground. It seemed as though we had entered a safe and dark nest.

We cleaned fallen apples off the ground, some larger than my fist, and rolled our sleeping bags out in six inches of lush, soft grass. It was as soft as a feather mattress.

We lay parallel to each other, separated by the trunk of the tree. I would have fallen to sleep in seconds, but Carl had gained a second wind and wanted to talk.

He began about how the people on the road now were ignorant of the most basic tramp ways. Earlier that summer he was traveling across Montana and came across some tramps who complained that they were out of food. "Why, I looked at them people like they were stupid," he said. "That whole flat out there was covered with nothing but wild mustard. All you had to do—they had a five-gallon bucket—was to wash them up, out them in a bucket, add salt and cook it. And you got greens. Some of the best greens you can eat! Just like spinach—same thing. So I gave them a little square of salt and says: 'There, go get yourself some of those wild mustard leaves and boil them up.' 'Ahhh, that's no good!' he answers. 'Go try it!' I says. So they went out and got arms full—you know, they pressed them down and boiled them, and almost filled that five-gallon bucket. Why, they ate that and they was goin' out to get some more!

"Yeah, you'd be surprised what you'd eat if you got hungry enough. Army taught me that. Frogs, worms, mice and rats, crickets, ants . . ."

"I ain't hungry enough yet," I said.

"Chinamen eat it," Carl said, "and consider it a delicacy. Dogs, cats . . . Indians in this country eat it. Meat's meat—all them tastes are just developed. Rabbit, turtle, snake—well, hell, a chicken is just about the dirtiest thing there is! You just ain't been hungry enough to have to look hard for food. You can barbecue any kind of meat and you would never recognize it! People walk around food, through, over, and under it, and never see it. Cracked wheat, for instance, is just wheat with the chaff busted off. You saw what was layin' around the yard? Hell, I was getting paid by the railroad to pick it up! That's the whole kernel—the chaff's busted off when it's harvested. See, they bleach it, the wheat flour, to make white bread. And you know white flour has no food value whatsoever. Your wheat bread has everything there—the whole kernel. And when the farmer sells his wheat they dock him if it's bleached. And then they turn around and bleach it themselves."

Carl told me about a book he'd read about how Minneapolis had changed from a lumbering and flourmilling town to a manufacturing center and he said: "Now they're tearing the hell out of skid row. Who do you think cut down those trees . . . worked that grain? It was the tramp, that's who. *We* built the railroad—that's why James J. Hill said: 'Put an empty on every train that leaves for the hobo to ride'—he wasn't being nice—he knew it couldn't have been done without the tramp. But now it's all forgotten. There's no place for our kind and they'll eliminate us like they'll eliminate the skid row. And it ain't just Minneapolis, it's every city in the west.

"It used to be Minneapolis was a good tramp town. I would've stayed this time except that getting out—that's the only way to sober up! If I'd stayed in town I could get all I wanted to drink—I'm seventy dollars in the hole now!"

"I guess that must be a difficult decision to make strung out on liquor."

"Not difficult at all. I had to take off. If I go broke on the road, I'll sober up. I won't be able to get it, and I won't bum for it!"

"That's the difference, isn't it . . . Those that will bum for the drink," I began.

"I won't bum for a drink. No . . . I'll give a guy a drink, if he bums me, but I can't do it myself—I just can't do it . . . Or to walk in the store and beg for something. No way! I'll go and ask them for a reduced price—like at a bakery store. I'll go in and ask if they have day-old stuff I can buy at half price—and nine times out of ten I'll get it!

"Or I'll offer to work—I've done that many a time. I'll see something that needs to be done and I need money; I'll go right up and ask them. I've done that a lot. And you'd be surprised at how many jobs I get, too. You walk up to these nice homes and see somebody out there lookin' . . . You know what they're thinkin'. I'll walk up to them: 'Hey, do you want that done? I'll do it for you.' 'Well, what do you charge?' I tell them a couple of bucks an hour and it's 'Why, *sure*.' Nine times out of ten I got two or three days work. Plus a meal or two. They'll always invite you in for a coffee and donut—fix you a lunch at noon. Then, if you're a good worker, they'll call up the neighbor and pretty soon you've got plenty of work—all it is is patience and a little effort, hell, anybody can do it. I've seen it a lot, you know, you'll see an old shaggy lawn that looks like it needs cuttin'—you'll see that man out there scratchin' his head or sittin' on the porch lookin' at it—it's easy to see he don't want to do it! But then he'll sit out there and watch you do it with a beer in his hand!

"The only time it was hard to find work was during the depression—there was no work—no money whatsoever. There were camps, like, called "Hoover Towns" where you could find food.

"I was just a young kid. Folks lost the farm for back taxes early in the depression—that's how a lot of the farms in Minnesota and Wisconsin got big, they bought up their neighbors for back taxes . . .

"See, I'm from Long Prairie—I was born in Long Prairie. That's west of Minneapolis a hundred miles; it's just a dinky little cow town. Retired farmers, dairy, that's about all. I haven't been there in, shit, forty years. I wouldn't know anybody there any more. I did go visit there once when I was in the service. I went to see some of the kids I grew up with. I remembered them and they remembered me. Just as soon as I came to the door: 'You got that Schmidt face!'—see, I got my mother's face.

"So we lost the farm, and then we lost the old man. He took off—hit the road. I never seen him again. I heard about him—I was in the service and they'd write: 'Well, we saw the old man in the street—drunk.' But I guess he's workin' somewhere, he's a good molder—ah, he's probably dead by now, Christ . . ." His voice dropped, and I asked:

"How old were you then?"

"Me, Christ, when he left I was about twelve . . . eleven, something like that. There was a whole family. Roland's the oldest—Betty's older, I'm the third oldest and there are four younger than me. Seven—shit, in the depression we couldn't get food. We didn't even have lights in our house! We moved into town, and then they put me on a farm. I think the only ones that stayed with my mother was the two youngest ones, Marlene and Edna. And today Marlene's a preacher. With my mother all the time—goody, goody—she turned into a minister.

"Room and board, that's all I got. Of course, I got my school, my clothes and don't worry—I had to work! They started payin' me wages, let's see, I guess I was fifteen. The year I started high school. They paid me ten dollars a month but I had to buy a bicycle and my clothing. I couldn't see the money—I couldn't have the money. So that's all I got was the same thing, only I got a bicycle! For that summer's work, and I worked like a man. Doin' pretty near the same work then as I do now. Pitch hay, milk cows, cultivate corn, plow, mow hay; everything. It was all horse and buggy in those days—no power of any kind. Kerosene lantern to milk the cows with, and I had to ride five miles one way to school.

"But I liked high school. And eighth grade of grade school. Because the people I was livin' with—their daughter was a teacher. I had to like it! I made good grades because she made me study—that's when I got interested in reading. And they started me in high school, and I was supposed to go to college, but then came the war . . .

"Yeah, I rode that old bicycle through many a storm. Cold! I *pushed* it through snow drifts. I'd get up, still dark out. Go out and do the chores, come in and eat breakfast—and then I'd jump on my bicycle and go to school. And smell like a cow barn all day. At night, I'd come home, do chores, milk—well, we'd eat before we milked, then we'd go out to the barn. Then, I'd come in the house and do my studies. And I'd have to study my catechism. See, I was confirmed Lutheran. They were German, and they knew how to work—whew! Before you'd get into bed there would always be a glass of milk and a cookie or something—maybe a piece of cake.

"That's why, when I see some of these guys—the way they eat, the way they act—it disgusts me. That filthy talk, I don't like it. They're just filth, don't know how to think any different."

"When I look around," I said, "I see a lot of men who are finished up. Nothing left of them, it seems . . . but I might be seeing it wrong. The man on skid row *looks* so bad."

"They're just a shell. You see them on skid row—that's the true bum. Now your hobo, he will work. He will when he's got to. He'll go from place to place. The tramp is the one who looks for work—makes it his living and supports himself. But that bum, he's the worst. But up here it's all mixed up, especially this time of year. And it's bad, you probably don't realize. There's a lot of shootings, murders. When the money starts, that's when it all happens. When these guys start comin' in after they been pickin' for a week or two and they've got a couple of hundred in their pocket—that's when you've got to watch it—in all of these taverns and all of these jungles. They get to drinkin' and fighting, flashing that money, and then there'll be somebody with a knife. Usually the jackroller picks up the pieces. A lot die, and nobody keeps track of them up here. You're on your own."

Those were the last words I remember as I fell into a heavy sleep. Enough moonlight had made its way through the branches to illuminate my companion in a soft, dappled light. I remember him sitting cross-legged between two branches, again keeping watch.

12

When I awoke, Carl was going through his gear and getting ready to leave. I stumbled along after the tramp in the cold, wet pre-dawn, but when we arrived at the jungle I did my part of the morning's rituals. As had been the case I was not much interested in the fire until it had been built; not much interested in coffee until it was swirling around in the can, and willing to eat my beans cold. This morning, however, the tramp was unusually cheerful and tolerant—clean up and shave, stop grouching! We're here and there's a job waiting.

We were finishing our food when a 1961 Ford four-door sedan drove up to the jungle. The car approached too fast, as though the driver had not noticed us, and skidded to a stop showering us with sand and gravel. A huge and dirty man emerged from the driver's seat and was jabbering by the time he hit the ground.

He "wondered if he might use our fire," and without waiting for an answer spread the contents of a large paper sack of food on the hood of his car. He poured some runny fat into a castiron frying pan, added a stringy, grey piece of meat, then carelessly set the pan on the grill, nearly knocking our coffee into the fire. He added three eggs and a can of beans and stirred everything together with a dirty fork. Through the entire process he did not stop talking and I swore that he was either laced with speed or on his tenth cup of coffee. He was a disagreeable, offensive presence which Carl and I tried to ignore.

I began to disagree with something the tramp said and he turned, for the first time to face me squarely: "What? You calling me a liar?" I was about to "sort out our misunderstanding," or "clarify my views," when Carl stepped between us and steered the tramp into another topic. Later I realized Carl had probably saved me from the kind of explosive outbursts I had seen often on the road, an irrational and unpredictable sort of violence that I'd connected, until that incident, with the fast high of cheap wine.

Our rubber tramp ate like an animal, cutting huge hunks from his meat, squashing it up against eggs and beans and shoveling it all into his mouth. When he'd finished he threw his empty cans into the

95

littered landscape and put the hot and dirty pan in the grease-stained paper bag. Without breaking his speedy monologue he jumped back into his car and left in the manner he had come. The car spun away and Carl just shook his head slowly back and forth—the transgressions were too numerous to list. We finished our last cup of coffee and hiked toward town.

We passed the remains of a wrecked school bus, which Carl called a popular hotel for the riffraff of the area, and he left me to go prowl around on the inside of the bus. In five minutes he emerged triumphant with a dirty brown paper sack, exclaiming in what I'd have to call joyful tones: "Breakfast! Cornmeal mush for breakfast!" I told him he ought to be ashamed for stealing some old bum's food.

We walked on to the employment center—an old trailer in a gravel pit—by skirting the town and staying near the railroad tracks. We arrived before seven-thirty but the area was already crowded with men waiting for the office to open. At eight o'clock the men began milling near the front of the trailer where a sliding window and a small writing ledge had been installed. A man of about twenty-five was stationed inside the trailer, behind a glass window. The men lined up and began filing past the window, leaving their names, and soon the news filtered up the line like a cloud of numbing gas—the harvest was not yet begun—no hiring had yet taken place. When our turn came, Carl told the employment officer we'd come all the way across the country, which of course meant nothing, but the employment officer showed a spark of sympathy I did not expect. When we'd left our names we joined the men behind the trailer.

Dullness, heat, incredible boredom! The day and the days ahead loomed terribly bleak, unfathomably empty. There was suddenly no goal, no road to follow, no activity to pass the time—just the wait, the wait in the empty heat. The orchards just out of sight tempted us in the cruelest sort of way—the apples were cool, moist and delicious; the work of the harvest would be another means, a solid and promising means to any end we'd choose. But the gravel pit where we languished was a place without promise; a place where the time crawled by like the flies that strolled across our dirty skin. It was the low point, our nadir, but perhaps what I learned, again, was that the temper of my expectations was not appropriate on the road. The wait was as much a part of the tramp life as had been the two-thousand-mile road before.

We sat with a group that included many we had ridden with from Wenatchee. There was little activity—no storytelling; no banter. A quiet stoicism seemed to fall over the group. Some cleaned up in one way or another; two old men dry-shaved and I winced as the ancient razor scraped across leathery skin. The blacks and the Indians separated themselves, and in each jungle wine appeared, it seemed magically, and soon there emerged drunken, almost celebrative noise. Although the wine-release was a most serious breaking of norm, I couldn't help but wonder how many of those present in our jungle would have joined if the opportunity had presented itself.

I spent the day in depressed silence. Late in the afternoon, after all job prospects seemed spent, I could stand it no longer and walked to the town. I walked down deserted streets, along wide sidewalks that led by tall wooden store facades. There were bars in which subdued activity could be heard but the few stores seemed empty. The main street ended at a park that was dominated by a vintage surface-to-air missile aimed over the river like an ancient battlement. The park was dirty and littered, but I found a cool spot in the shade and lay down to collect my thoughts.

I realized that it was the first time I had taken myself from the immediate reality of tramp life; it was the first opportunity I'd had to seriously reflect upon what had taken place since I left Minneapolis.

I felt as though I'd gone through a fundamental change. A sociologist might say that I was "merging with my role," meaning simply that my inner world—my expectations, categorizations, "attitudes," or whatever one chooses to label normal thinking patterns—was coming into synchronization with an outward appearance I'd simply assembled with clothes, equipment, and passage into a particular environment. The trip thus differed radically from any previous one I'd had on freights or hitchhiking highways and could perhaps most aptly be described as an apprenticeship. I did not know if the apprentice/master roles were usual; I did feel that the tramp and I had both overstepped usual ways of being together on the road. He'd begun to make decisions for both of us and he'd told me much of his pre-tramp life. I'd sensed a gruff friendship coming from him and I'd responded with my own. But it would be wrong to describe the changes in our relationship as the result of calculation or of manipulation; rather, I believe we were merely letting our feelings for each other take their natural direction.

As Carl's buddy, sidekick, or pupil, however, I had begun to see the inner workings of a life I had only before observed on the surface. The understanding of the life included an appreciation, first, for the purposefulness rather than aimlessness that lay at the basis of the movement, the work, and even the drinking. These men were not "drifters." The life was a complicated, even intricate set of rules and expectations, and the different ways in which different men on the road followed the prescribed ways of behaving layered them into distinct groups. The rules were in some cases simple: ride this way or that on the freights; drink in one situation but not the next; work and work hard but never let an employer gain the sense of ownership over anything but the time he bought; and retain a constant guard over establishing anything but immediate, uncommitted yet not unserious relationships with others. It could thus be reduced to sets of rules and subrules, and the social stratification that then emerged around how well each group performed would take on a quite rigid quality; yet there were far more subtle realities to the life than such a view would include. I wondered in particular about the role played by alcohol. All identified the skid row man as a bum because he'd lost his control over alcohol, yet every one of them spent time incapacitated, abused, robbed and exploited on the back alleys of the mission strips during interludes from the road. The aversion of the tramps in the boxcar to the offered wine had been startling, coming as it did from men who had described their own uncontrolled drinking with essentially an acceptance, even humor. It was clear at least that skid row included more than people to whom alcoholic dependence had become a way of life; it included, as well, others for whom the experience was an episode on the way to other, very different experiences.

Nearly everyone was gone when I returned to the pit, and Carl seemed glad to see me and the groceries I had bought on the way. I'd bought a can of sardines to break the monotony of Campbell's "pork" and beans and the tramp chided me gently for wasting money on such extravagance.

We returned to the jungle where the late afternoon sun glinted off

98

the remains of ten thousand broken wine bottles. The seven upturned five-gallon cans around the remains of the fire projected the loneliness and desolation I felt, but soon some of the men from the jungle by the trailer arrived and brought with them a sense of camaraderie. Carl left to find the can he had stashed but someone had taken it during the day. I remember thinking that it had been odd to go through elaborate procedures to hide a tin can, and it seemed more unusual to have it stolen.

The old man called grandpa was building a fire. The others stretched out around him, and a quiet jesting began as they recounted the luck they'd had during the day. It was relaxed and it was friendly because the experience had made us all the same; for the others it was a repetition of a thousand moments, but for me it represented an acceptance I had not felt before.

Once again, the jungles were racially segregated. In ours there were no Indians or blacks, but a tall, thin Mexican tramp, carrying no gear and wearing colorful clothes, approached the group and said: "Where I come from they call me the 'Latin Lover'—yeah, they say: 'Here comes that fucking Mexican!' "—a line which drew a few laughs and smoothed his entry into the group.

The old man took a large aluminum pot and four metal pie tins from one of his gunny sacks and had begun to heat water in the pot. He dug deep into his other sack for a piece of meat which he cut into seven equal pieces. Carl contributed a can of beans and another tramp added a half a jar of navy beans. The mulligan was completed with carrots and cauliflower someone had picked up from behind a produce house, and then Carl salted and peppered the pot of food. The cooking was done with great ceremony while we all sat around joking and talking.

The stew was shared although some had contributed nothing. It struck me that people had shorted themselves to feed the group; this generosity seemed surprising in such a group of loners. The food appeared to be part of the experience of the wait for the harvest, and once again the experience was the great equalizer.

Some planned to catch the local freight to a town further north where it was easier to get foodstamps. They planned their run for the train, discussing the most likely place for the engineer to slow, and they cleared the most jagged rocks from their path. The old man

99

wanted to go along but I doubted whether he would be able to catch the freight, burdened and slow as he'd become.

The rest sat around the jungle fire, sipping coffee and telling stories. The evening jungle has a particular quality; the stories are told and retold, and the day's difficulties seem far behind. The group collectively buoys itself with its memories and the stories repeat a basic theme: the tramp as trickster—the tramp as the winner in a game whose rules he does not accept. I remember a story that could stand for all the rest: a tramp named Strawberry told of getting off a train by mistake in a small town in Utah where he learned that the next train was due in a week. Strawberry had been working and had a good amount of money which he stashed under some rocks behind the jungle and took just enough for his daily supplies when he went to town. The town policeman picked him up, as he had expected, but when he discovered the tramp had no money he didn't lock him up but told him to get out of town. Strawberry said he was just in town to get his supplies, so the police let him shop, but when he walked out of the grocery door with his case of beer and gallon of wine the cop was still there, waiting. As soon as the tramp sat down the cop motioned him to the car and took him the hell out of town, back to the jungle. The same thing happened the next day. After a couple of days, said Strawberry, that policeman was driving out to the jungle in the morning to pick him up, waiting while he bought his wine, and taking him back to the jungle—just to keep him out of sight. "Yeah," said Strawberry, "that was the nicest situation I've ever been in—but I thought that if I didn't pick up that freight when he came through that old cop might just change the color of his hat!"

I heard repeated what I'd learned from Carl—as long as one kept sight of one's independence very little could be genuinely threatening. Two tramps talked of riding freights to Florida to pick oranges and mentioned that it would be a tricky ride through Texas when the peas were being harvested—if they were caught, they'd spend a month and a half working for the state of Texas for no paycheck. But that possibility did not seem to discourage the tramps much; it certainly would not change their plans. For even of they were caught the detour would only be temporary. Their lives—the *life*—would go on; and if the life was based on anything it was on the feeling that one lived in the moment; one did not defer gratification; one did not base his happi-

100

ness and satisfaction on the accomplishing of abstract goals. This produced, I believe, both an intensity and a sense of relaxation. The most mundane of the day's possibilities became quite important but the overall questions of why they were in the life or what particular things might make their lives worse or better were not of much interest. That night the most important thing was telling stories and the stories were quite good indeed.

When the sound of the northbound train was heard, some of the storytellers broke in midsentence to gather their gear and run to the tracks. As the train rounded the corner I could see dark shapes hanging out of the boxcar doors. Two whistles sounded and the men flew off the train, while at nearly the same instant, others tried to board. The old man never had a chance—by the time he was running jerkily along the tracks the train was already picking up speed. I saw him look over his shoulder at a boxcar rushing toward him and for a moment I thought he would try to swing into its open door. He seemed poised to make the jump and then backed off and I was relieved, for I was certain that if he had jumped he would have gone onto the rocks, or under the wheels.

The men who jumped the train disappeared quickly. None except the old man approached our fire. He limped back, disgusted with himself, and said: "They're getting thick around here! If you shook a bush there'd be three goddamn tramps fallin' out!" And then he left us and walked south, away from most of the people. Carl said he had too much gear and someone would get him one day or the next, and while I admired the tenaciousness with which he clung to his life, I saw too that it had become a hard road.

13

We waited until late into the evening to make our way back into the orchard. The tramp sat quietly for a few minutes, then said:

"You learned quite a few tricks today . . . Pretty soon you'll know what the hell you're doing on this road. You listen to that Angler Joe—he knows what he's talking about. You learned how to break a bottle so there a piece sharp enough to shave with, and he showed you how to open a tin can by rubbing it on a flat rock. Even knowing how to boil water in a bottle—there's always a bottle around a jungle—might make the difference between whether or not you have your coffee!" Carl chuckled. "Yep, old Angler Joe. I knew I knew him. He used to hang around with old Dirty Hands, and a guy they called 'Porkchops.' I told you about Porkchops, didn't I?

"Old Porkchops used to live with the rats down in Wishram below the dump. Wishram is the first division going south out of Pasco. Anyway, he got his pension and they cleaned him up, and dressed him up—made him stop livin' with those damn rats, and he died—he just couldn't change. 'Course he fucked himself up eatin' garbage for forty years . . .''

"I wonder what they thought of me tonight," I said, "there's not many my age. I got the impression that if I hadn't been with you, I wouldn't have been very welcome in that jungle."

"They wouldn't accept you alone. These guys know me, and well, if I accept you, they will."

"But there's a lot of things different about me. You had to tell them I bought sardines! They got a good laugh out of that! And I would have washed my clothes in that laundromat, if I wouldn't have thought they'd all laugh at me!"

"No, you're wrong. They do the same thing if they had the money. The tramp would, that is, not the bum. You seen them wasting money on liquor and candy and foolishness. And then you saw the others shaving and cleaning up this morning. It'll make a difference! You got to be as clean as you can get to get that job! If you're dirty that farmer will look at you: 'Well, I don't want you . . .' You can tell the working man, you can tell him real easy. You saw the way that employment agent treated us—he knew we meant business. And he knows Haskel, Burns and Kernin . . ."

"If you can get a job for yourself, then get it—we don't have to stay together!"

"No, no. See, I quit him twice already this year. I don't want to go up there the way things sit between us. Don't worry—I'd'a gone there first if I thought anything good would have come of it . . . and I might have taken you along. Shit, we could have had a cabin right now! Those are good cabins, too. It's up close to the border, last place on the line. Up to Womack on the freight, then hitchhike, or walk—it's about forty miles from there. Used to be a local, but he don't run anymore. No, there's no reason to go up there—we'd just be wasting our time. All these places will start about the same time.

"Shit, that's a nice moon out there," the tramp said after a few moments. The moon was just over the horizon, orange and round. "Harvest moon," he said.

"You know I was walking around town today and people were pretty nice to me."

"It's a nice little town," Carl agreed.

"People were nodding to me, saying hello, saying, 'Up to pick a few apples? Well, I hope you have a good stay! Little early yet . . .' "

"They see that money comin'. Sure, they'll be nice to you. If you're sober and behave yourself, they won't bother you a bit."

"Some night we got to go in that tavern and not get loaded," I said. "Just look around, see what's happening."

"I been in 'em. I know what's happening. I ain't got nothin' to learn sitting in a fuckin' tavern."

I let it drop. Perhaps as much as anything he could say his response pointed to the reality that underlay the relationship between the tramp and me. We shared our experience, and we shared it equally. But we were frozen in in one stage of a sequence of events. I was asking the tramp to leave that sequence, to step outside his own experience to accompany me as I observed another part, probably a painful part of his life, as it was being lived by others. I could not imagine the tramp not in control, but it was clear that *he* could, and it was not something he wished to be reminded of.

"You know," I said a few minutes later, "I was talking to a woman today in town that knew one of the owners. So I asked her, 'What do

103

the owners think of the guys that come here to pick?' And she said that the owner distinguished between the ones that come here to work and the ones that come here to raise trouble. She said that the town was locked up tight against the bums in this town itself, not against the men migrating in that wanted to work. The owner she was describing had lost a lot of irrigation pipe that year and didn't blame the men who had come into town. Now, that's what they say."

"Oh, yeah, that's the townspeople doing that. What in hell would a tramp want with irrigation pipe? It's the townspeople, thinking they can get by with it now that the migrants are filling up the streets. Well, hell, I'll tell you something—the guy I worked for up in Oroville, Frank, he's a deputy. Most of these guys are deputies. Well, do you know what their main job is now? Goin' up and riding the hills for cattle rustlers. It's the homeguard goin' up there, shootin' cows. Butcher 'em themselves. Beef's gone so goddamn high they can't afford it."

I asked Carl to define a "homeguard."

"That's a tramp expression," Carl answered. "That's what they call a man who lives in town. He doesn't travel, he lives in that town steady. There's no tramps called homeguards . . .

"If he's a homeguard, he's no tramp, no hobo, no bum . . . Well, he might be a bum. But he's no tramp or no hobo. He could even be a homeowner. He's probably a guy that just never really made it in the town. You might call him a town bum, or a homeguard, but he's still a bum. That's why a migrant worker, when he goes into town and goes to the employment office gets mad because he can't get a job, and he sees everybody else getting one. It's always the homeguard, the one that lives there that gets the first job, see. Naturally a town is going to do that, because they are their own people. So the tramp will cuss out the homeguard, the one who has been stayin' there."

"Is the tramp who travels for twenty or thirty years, then settles down, a homeguard?"

"If he gets his pension and don't work, then he's just an ex-tramp. But if he gets off the road, or off the tramp, and settles down and takes a job in the town, then he's a homeguard . . . Oh, it's funny, you know, it's just our lingo."

"There were a lot of things said today that I didn't understand," I commented. "A lot of terms about trains I don't know very well."

"Most of that stuff just comes natural after a while. But the rail lingo is dyin' out. These fellas don't use it any more. It ain't like it was. You tell a guy there's a 'hot rail'—he don't even know what you're talkin' about."

"Is that a hotshot?"

"A hot *rail*."

"A hot yard?"

"No, a hot rail."

"Okay, what's that?" I asked.

"A train comin' down the track. When it's in sight you call it a 'hot rail.' But I don't even think of those things no more. It's dyin' out. The new tramps is different. They act different, they look different, and they talk different."

"That may be," I said, "but as long as there's fruit there'll be tramps here to harvest it. And as long as there are trains there'll be people riding. So you would think that the lingo wouldn't die out, and that the people would still be tramps."

"Well, there'll be different guys. And it *is* going downhill. Now it's a different class of people. And eventually there's not going to be a train you can ride. They're building the cars so you can't ride 'em. It's not that they're cracking down in the yards—they'll have cars after a while where there's no space where you can get in."

"You mean they won't cart empties around?"

"Well, if they do, they close them up! Like that one we couldn't get into. They seal 'em."

"But you can break those seals easy enough . . ."

"You better not break that seal! You won't go breaking no seals if you know what's good for you. Interstate commerce regulations. You'll really get your ass in trouble if you go fucking around with those seals. See, if one seal's already broken, you're all right. But they're startin' to seal both sides. You can't tell where the empties are. Are you telling me you're going to walk down that train and break seals until you find an empty? I'll stand back and watch—you tell me when you find one!"

"You could always ride a gondola, couldn't you?"

"They're covering the gondolas, too. Don't you remember seeing some of those on the tracks?"

"Well, how about the piggybacks?"

105

"You know on a piggyback, you only have to have just enough floor space for the wheels of the truck. They're starting to build them without no floor in them . . . You can't ride 'em! Just a runway for the truck wheels to go on."

"But what about grain cars?"

"They're building them without floors too! Just a little framework—no floor at all. *No*body can crawl in there and hang on. Maybe for ten miles, but that's it. And if you fall through one of those, you know where you're going, don't you? Under the wheels!

"And those grain cars with the solid steel floor? You get in the back there—that's a damn good ride in the summer, but in the wintertime—you can't do it! Anything in steel in the winter—you stay off it . . . unless you can put two or three layers of cardboard between you and the steel, then you might be able to make it. But I've been so cold I couldn't move! Sitting on some steel floor of some boxcar, too cold to move, thinkin' if I don't move, I'll never get up. Christ, that's cold!

"And they're getting faster and faster. Used to be highball meant about fifty miles an hour . . . That was back in the steam days. Now the only thing that's keeping them under ninety is the tracks. When they get around to fixin' the tracks, it'll be all over . . . Nobody can ride 'em when they go like that.

"It's all going downhill," he continued after a long pause. "The oldtimer wouldn't have nothing to do with this bunch. He'd a gone off by himself. Built his own fire. If you go and see him, you know what he'd do? Hand you a match. He won't say a word, he'd just hand you a match. You know what that means, don't you? . . . Go light your own fuckin' fire!

"I had one pull that on me in Avery, Idaho. It was when I rode the old Milwaukee—I was a gandy dancer in them days, yeah, I had my rockin' chair made . . . I had my rockin' chair made. But what that tramp didn't know was that I was carryin' my packsack, a bedroll, a chucksack and everything! Fishin' gear . . . I just walked over to him, lookin' for a campsite. You know, to go fishin', it's good fishin' there—over the mountains in Idaho. He just walked over and handed me a match—I just looked at him—*I* knew what he was doing. I stuck the match in my pocket and walked away. I got up wind of him and built my camp. It was pretty early in the morning and I could see that he didn't have nothin' to eat . . ."

106

"Do you mean if you had walked up there with your gear he would have been glad to see you?"

"If I'd had my gear it would have been all right. So I threw bacon on the pan; see, I went upwind so that the smell would blow right to him. I threw my bacon in the pan and a little while later he raised his head up, just like that! Sniff, sniff! I cooked my bacon up good—I peeled my potatoes, put them in there . . . God *damn,* he wanted to eat! 'Course he'd never come up then . . ."

"It appears to me," I said, "that it's all the same, but it's moved down a notch. The tramps you describe wouldn't associate with the tramps in our jungle, but the tramps in our jungle didn't associate with different groups today around the employment office."

Carl answered: "The real tramp of twenty years ago wouldn't associate with the real tramps that are around today for the same reasons that nobody was goin' over to those two jungles at the trailer. It ain't because they're blacks and Indians—well, maybe it's because they're blacks and Indians, but mostly it is because they were drunk and filthy. But what you're driving at is true: it's become a less honorable profession."

"But it still confused me," I said. "My impression, which is an outsider's impression, is that you people tend to do more of exactly what you want than most people I've met, but maybe I'm romanticizing."

"No, no! That's why we live like this—this is why we're on the road," Carl interrupted.

"The thing that I see that makes you different from most I've met on the road is that you're free of the bottle, again, most of the time."

"If you don't, you turn into a bum," Carl said slowly. "Any time you start depending on that bottle, buddy, you better go to a doctor. Or the AA, one or the other. 'Cause then you're an alcoholic. You lose your packsack, your bedroll, your gear—you lose everything you got. Then all you got is the clothes on your back and you become a bum.

"But most aren't like that. You heard that one guy—he said they can stop drinkin' when they go to jail! Which is true. They can also stop drinkin' when they go broke. In other words, they said right out they won't bum a drink. Or they won't bum a bottle. A drink is different. They'll go to the bartender where they spend their money and get an eye-opener—or maybe one bottle—that's reasonable. Or go to a place

107

where they buy their booze for a loan. That's what I did this last time, and that's the third time! Every time I go back there I owe him money, and I always give it to him, right off."

"If he were really looking after your welfare he wouldn't give you that money," I said, and the tramp snorted: "Are you crazy? He's in that business! You multiply me by, say, five hundred guys, and you can imagine the business he's got. Joe ain't broke, he's got a beautiful home out there on Lake Minnetonka. That seventy dollars? That's like a drop in the bucket. Don't worry, he'll loan me the money. He's afraid of losing the customer. He knows I'll pay, but he won't do that for a wino."

"No?"

"Uh-uh," Carl answered, "not on your life. He might give him one pint, or if he's a good customer, one fifth. After that, no-no."

"When I used to hang around the skid row in Boston," I said, "down on Sunday morning they'd be bumming—I know I'm an easy mark, they never pass me up."

"Then you're just as bad as that liquor store owner that loaned me the seventy! If you didn't give them the money, they couldn't get drunk!"

I said, "But back in Boston, these skid row alcoholics would have to buy from a bootlegger on Sunday. They'd have to pay twice the price for their wine. Why couldn't they put a bottle up for Sunday?"

"Same in Minneapolis," Carl answered, "same on every skid row in the country. Eighty-five-cent bottle of wine will cost you two dollars on Sunday. That's a pint! There's no such thing as a fifth on Sunday morning—they don't sell it; nobody has that much money!

"But they try to do that, like you said, take a bottle, even two, to bed with them on Saturday. They wake up: 'Damn, all my wine's gone! What happened to my wine!' They drank it up, of course. They get so befuddled they don't know what they do. So they'll go up and down the street and bum every person they see. Their friends, enemies, *women,* anybody. They're desperate! They know what's around the corner and it ain't a pretty picture. You get dehydrated, go into the DT's—man—it'll stop your heart from pumping!

"I worked in Cook County, Chicago. I stayed there for ninety days—I hit a queer that wouldn't leave me alone. Down at Robert E. Rothschild's down on skid row on Madison Street, Chicago. Three

108

times I moved from that guy. Each time I told the bartender: 'If he's goin' to fuck with me, I'm goin' to knock him on his ass!' . . .'Oh,' says the bartender, 'he'll be all right, he'll be all right.' So the third time he did it, pow! And as I hit him the cops come walkin' in the door. Off to jail I go! Ninety days in the slammer! But that guy wouldn't appear against me, he knew he was wrong. It took me ninety days to get out of that coop they kept me in. Once a week they'd bring me to that judge and they'd keep postponing the case because the guy wouldn't appear. Ninety days they kept me; well, they kept me workin' up at the night hospital. One of my jobs at night was to stuff the corpses when they die. And watch them die. They came off of *skid row*—too far gone on alcohol, there's nothing left. The doctors would shoot 'em—they'd give them that—what is it? Famaldahyde, or remaldahyde, one or the other, and the next fuckin' thing I'd go over and they'd be stiffer'n a door. Two a day, at least . . .

"And we'd have to strap them down—they'd go out of their mind. If you ever saw a man in the DT's you gotta expect the strength of ten men. They pretty near go crazy! Christ, they would grab hold of your hand and as strong as you are, you can't pry their fingers loose!

"You have to strap their hands down, and their ankles, and you put a sheet across their chest. A sheet across their knees to keep them in bed. The fight! And before the morning comes—they're dead. And if you know Cook County you know they don't give a damn. Tie their hands, tie their feet. Close their eyes and stuff their ass—tie a whatchamacallit around their prick—then roll 'em up in what we call thousand-mile paper. Next morning the truck would come and haul them off. Tie a cord around their jaw to keep their mouth shut, for rigor mortis. Sometimes the looks on their faces . . . they'd haunt you . . . I'd dream about it . . . them sons-of-bitches coming after me . . ."

We let the fire die out and sat silently in the darkness. When Carl was sure there wasn't anybody around, we headed back to the overgrown part of the orchard. We walked quietly through the long grass until Carl picked out a tree where we could sleep. The full moon lit our way and the night was full of shadows.

Days passed much like the first. We survived on cornmeal, a few beans, odd stews made with food scrounged here and there. Tramps moved through our jungle, but it remained much the same. A monotony crept in; I began to lose track of time and I ceased noting conversations or writing much at all. It was as though we were all on hold . . . the slowly ripening apples holding the key to our transition.

It finally came to an end late one afternoon. We were sitting by the trailer when the agent pointed to Carl and me, and a soft-spoken man leaning against a sixty-nine Chevy pickup motioned for us to come over and throw our gear in the back of his truck. It was that simple; we told him our names and shook hands; he asked us if we could pick and then we crowded into his pickup and drove a few miles out of town to the orchard. We were about the first from our jungle to go.

14

The beginning of work marked the end of a distinct phase in my relationship with the tramp. We were suddenly no longer dependent on my money, and as we left the life of tramping and began working Carl had less and less to teach me, less to lead me through. It was during those days that he withdrew more and more, and I felt as though he believed he had said too much, revealed more than he wanted known.

But the first night in the cabin we shared a mood of celebration. The cabin was about twelve feet square with a table, two cots, stove and a sink. We cooked a little food we'd been saving, sat looking at each other across the table and the tramp said it was about time he started living right again.

He said: "When you start drinkin' you don't eat right. Maybe one meal a day—at the most."

I told him I didn't understand that kind of a binge because when he woke up he'd be sober—maybe hungover, but sober. He interrupted: "No-no. I wake up a dozen times a night! I wake up, take a drink! In the beginning of a drunk I'll wake up a dozen times. Only later, when I get used to it again—then I don't have to wake up no more. I can stay drunk through the night."

"But at some point in those weeks you make a decision—made a decision to get through with it."

110

Carl chuckled at me and said: "Why sure! When I was down to my last hundred and fifty, I says, 'Oh, oh! Carl's goin' to have to go!'"

"Do you carry all that in cash?" I asked.

"Sure."

"That's stupid. That's really stupid. I can't believe you walk around drunk for weeks with that kind of money in your pocket."

"Nobody knew I had it," Carl answered.

"People roll drunks to find out!"

"That may be," Carl said, "but I still bet you couldn't find it. I don't carry it in a big lump of bills—I carry it in hundred-dollar bills. Three or four of them don't take up much room."

"But you got to *cash* those things." I groaned, half-kidding: "It makes my heart sick to think of you drinking up three hundred and fifty dollars in a week!"

Carl laughed: "Did I tell you about earlier this spring? Fifteen hundred!"

"Fif-teen hundred!"

"But it took me most of a month," Carl replied. "Well, I worked most all winter for Lundstrom's there in Minneapolis.

"When I drink like that I stay in hotels," Carl explained. "Steak dinners, seven, eight dollars just for myself. And the hotel will cost me twelve or fifteen dollars a night—I go first class, man!"

I shook my head, and Carl continued: "I flew out here last time . . . And when I fly I always fly first class. That's free drinks and free meals, but there's a limit to how much you can absorb in that much time."

"Fif-teen hundred dollars!" I repeated, mostly to myself.

Carl continued: "Well it should cost, I stayed in the Coeur d'Alene Hotel—that ain't no cheap joint! I sat in the cocktail lounge all day, and their steak costs like hell. Yeah, I just signed the check . . . I didn't carry the money with me that time."

"Did you plan to do that when you were working?" I asked.

"Why sure—that's my vacation! I worked all winter; I worked like hell—I didn't drink pretty near all winter. So what the hell!"

"I'm not passing judgment," I said, "but for crying out loud . . ."

"I know what you're thinking," Carl said, "you're thinking: 'What could I do with that kind of money!'"

"Maybe—maybe—I just don't know. I guess I never had fifteen

111

hundred in my hand. If I had it, I guess I'd put it down on some land."

Carl replied: "What are you going to buy—three acres? Then lose it for taxes because you ain't got enough to keep payin' for it? You want me to work for the next seven or eight years to finish it up and then how old am I—fifty-eight?— pretty near ready for the grave. So who's goin' to get the benefit? No, I do want a piece of ground—not expensive—some place I can build a cabin—next to a creek. Where I can relax and do some fishin' and sit by myself, that's *by myself,* so I can get away from everything and everybody. So I know that nobody's going to come on that land unless I invite them!"

"Well, Carl, that's what a lot of us talk about. What the hell, I guess it's not my place to say . . . You seem to be doing what you want."

"What tee's me off is this in-between!" Carl said. "When I'm not drinkin' or not workin'. Like now, see, this last one. Now that was a boo-boo—that was really a screw-up. 'Cause that was three hundred and some dollars over there, and not long before that another five hundred up here on another one . . . That's pretty near a thousand bucks! Now, if I was on the ball, I'd have that thousand saved, plus what I could have been makin' when I was gone, layin' drunk in the gutter—and now with what we are goin' to make pickin'—why, you heard what the man said—you can work up here until it snows, and then you pick props. And then when the weather moderates a little you go to prunin'. Now I had the job sewed up. I'm off at the most two months a year. And in a couple of years I'd have that place and I wouldn't have to work no more. In, say, five years. By then I'd be able to draw my social security; be able to work when I wanted to. Like in thinnin' or pickin'—that'd be all I'd have to work!"

"Are you going to do it, Carl?"

His mood changed and he laughed at himself. "Now I save penny-penny-penny; when I get drunk I spend dollars-dollars-dollars!"

"This is what I'm trying to understand," I said, "all this contradiction. What stands between what you are and what you want. For instance, right now I'd like to go to a tavern and spend an evening drinking, but I don't want to start you on a goddamned drunk!"

"How long do you think an evening consists of?" Carl asked.

"For me it consists of when I go in until the bar closes. There's a certain amount of good times to be had going into a bar on Saturday night and getting loaded."

"Not around here," Carl replied. "Like I said, when I left here the last time I got out of this country before I drank. They don't know who you are if you leave, but around here they know damn well who you are and what you're up to. And that'll get you into trouble. I've gotten enough goods taken off me to know that.

"You can't be too careful. Last time it was two dollars and ten dollars worth of groceries. That's where I got this scar." He pointed to his face and I tried to pick just one crease but couldn't; I just nodded and thought what it would be like to get slashed across the face with a broken bottle while sleeping in the weeds.

We talked about the job that lay ahead. We were a little worried about not screwing it up. Carl said: "It's no different than any of the jobs I've had. You've got to work hard and do what the boss says. Do you know I'll be fifty years old this winter and that in all my life I've never had trouble getting a job? That is because I leave a good name behind me, wherever I go. I just won't give up! And do you know who taught me this? When my folks, my mother, sent me away from her—'cause my dad disappeared, you know—to that farm, why, those farmers like to have worked me to death! Like an animal. To them I was just another animal to pull a load. And, that's how I was trained. Work till you dropped. I never got over it . . . I'll work till I can't work no more, until I just can't straighten up—you wait until tomorrow and see how much time I'll take at lunch. When I say I'm going to work twelve hours, I'll work twelve hours."

We bedded down early and though it was good to be inside I would have traded the sagging mattress on the rickety cot for the soft grass under a tree. At four in the morning I was restless and went for a walk. Coyotes howled from hills I could barely see. I went back to the cabin but couldn't sleep and rose quickly when the alarm, supplied with the cabin, rang at five. Just as in the boxcars and the weeds, Carl sat bolt upright at the first sound.

We had a long breakfast of corn meal mush and coffee and then the foreman gave us picking bags, ladders and small books in which we'd keep track of our work. It was still almost dark, and the apples, larger than my fist, were wet with dew. The branches, even with propping,

113

bent all the way to the ground. We were assigned to pick different parts of the orchard but both began in the golden delicious—soft, yellow apples that bruised easily. I quickly filled the bag which hung from my shoulders to my knees, then bent over a bin, unhooked the sack, and carefully let the apples roll out. If the apples rolled too hard they would bruise. If they were pulled off the branches instead of twisted off—then gently tipped until they came undone, finger marks—small bruises—would be left on the apples. And if they were twisted too hard the stems would pull out of the apple and remain on the tree, and the foreman told us that *nobody* wanted apples without stems.

Alone in the orchard, although within hearing distance of other pickers I had not yet met, I climbed to the top of my twelve-foot ladder to eat an apple and survey the barren land in the colors of dawn. Nothing but prairie sage grew on the small round mountains that rose on either side of the orchard. The river valley had been irrigated and planted, and along the flat areas above the river a green swath cut through the brown landscape. I watched the hills change from soft grays to a slight golden color, and then to a color between rose and brown. The sun finally beamed over the mountain, beginning the day with harsh light. Between six-thirty and eight in the morning the apples were cold and wet but the work was good.

All morning I worked along a row of trees, seeing only the foreman and his wife who drove tractors and moved bins. The foreman had a flat-top haircut, a clean shave and a cowboy shirt. He called me by my first name and spoke with a long drawl.

At noon I went back to the cabin for some lunch and a rest. I had not seen Carl all morning and he didn't come back to eat. Then I worked until the foreman told me it was five o'clock. I was pretty happy with my first day's work until the owner came by to tell me that I'd bruised a lot of apples and I better slow down until I got the hang of it. I met Carl on the way back to the cabin and he told me, gloating a little, that he'd picked two bins more than I had, and that nobody had been by to tell him his apples had been bruised. He'd drawn his first day's pay and arranged a ride into town with the owner to buy food. We spent most of Carl's twenty on hamburger and bread, canned vegetables, potatoes, eggs, onions, peanut butter and margerine. I wanted some cheese and lettuce but Carl said that cheese

114

made his stomach hurt and lettuce was for rabbits. We also bought a couple of pie tins for plates and a couple of utensils so we could eat at the same time. Carl picked up a chocolate cream pie which really seemed out of character and I added a six-pack of beer which drew no comment.

Back in the cabin Carl was in an unusually good mood, saying things like: "You can't live out of tin cans like we've been forever!" I took a shower in a stall outside and enjoyed the feeling of losing a couple of layers of dirt. By the time I'd finished, Carl had supper ready—hamburger mashed up with onions and ketchup.

"What did I tell you?" Carl said after we'd eaten, "did you see me in here for lunch?"

"No, I sure did not. You're crazy."

"How many bins did you get today?" Carl asked again.

"Four."

"I got five and a half. See, there you are."

"Like I said, you're crazy. Life's too short to work with you."

"How would you like to work eighty-nine and a half hours with me?" I didn't answer.

"Do you know what I do in the harvest, when I'm working on a tractor? I don't stop. I eat my lunch on the ride."

"Ugh!"

"The only time I stop is to put fuel in it!"

"We're made out of different material," I said; "I work hard, but I don't work that hard."

"Go on a wreck with me some day," Carl said, "there's where you make your money—"

"—But two lousy bucks an hour," I interrupted.

"Wait a minute now . . . how much do you figure a motel costs these days? . . . And it costs them anywhere from seven to eight dollars a day just for your food."

"Not that much," I answered.

"Yes it does! How much do you think a breakfast is?"

"Buck, buck and a half!"

"You got to have some food to work all day! Can't get that for a buck and a half! What do you think lunch costs?"

"Buck, buck and a half."

"Oh, shit," Carl snorted, "you must be crazy! You're not going to

115

work hard on a dollar and a half—you might get a sandwich. I'm talking about chicken, or steak, or chops—two and a half, or two seventy-five. So you figure it out. If you work fifteen hours that's thirty dollars. Plus the fifteen it costs for room and board, that's forty-five. You make forty-five dollars right there."

"Fifteen hours! For Christ's sake, Carl . . . people are talking about a thirty-hour *week*!"

"Thirty hour week, my foot! That's baloney, bullshit. There ain't never going to be a thirty hour week for that work. You might get *sixty*. You might get away with sixty and think that you're lucky.

"The week before that, I got sixty-one and a half hours. I made a hundred and twenty-three dollars. The last week I made a hundred and seventy-nine dollars. So you figure it out. And I was stayin' in the yards on Nicollet Island—that didn't cost me nothin'."

"I've heard that Nicollet Island is one rough place," I said.

Carl answered: "It isn't to the tramps. And the bums won't hurt you. It's the other people—the niggers and the hippies—if they see you down there they'll kill you! . . . I just don't know what's happened to Minneapolis, it used to be a friendly town. Not no more. Too many aimless young people. It's the young people that are beatin' up on the destitute, you know. It's not the university students. I never seen a university student come down there, except to the army surplus store, the same place that I shop."

"When I was fifteen years old," I began, "I had a friend that was ten years older, and he stayed with me one summer. He'd take me down there and say: 'Here's the other side of life . . .'"

"He didn't know what he was talkin' about," Carl interrupted. "He saw that, that's all—the bums lined up along the streets. They think that's it . . . that all the guys that ride up and down the road are just like those guys on Hennepin—which is just not true!"

"I'm beginning to learn that," I said, "if all your stories are true, which it seems they are after today, you're the hardest working sonofaguns . . ."

"*Bitches*," Carl corrected me, "'one of the hardest working sonofabitches you ever saw. And I could take you to Minneapolis and show you fifty guys just like me. They might look like bums or derelicts, but they're workers. You thought being a tramp meant being just a no-good—well, I hope I've showed you, showed you how to tell the working men from the rest. Their clothes and their gear. You got to look at their hands; their hands give it away every time." He held his hands out. "What do you think made my hands like that? Where do you think I got the big knuckles?"

"Sticking them in the wrong place?"

"Sticking—you come pretty close," Carl said. "Sticks, what are sticks?"

"Lumber?"

"Lumber, that's another name for it. We used to make money in Chicago, see, we were "extra-gang labor" in those days. We were drawing "rocking-chair," what we called rocking-chair which is unemployment insurance from the railroad . . . Do you know what we'd do on a different social security number? We'd stack lumber. Not the kind you're thinkin'—we'd go to the bowling alley and set pins. And do you know how much those pins weigh?

"I've set as many as a hundred and seventy-five lines in one night! I can still scoop that ball yet and throw it . . . Pick up three pins in each hand, but they don't have that anymore—it's all automatic. Well, that's what made my fingers grow crooked.

"See, you grab them like this," Carl continued, "one here, between the thumb and forefinger, another right next to it and the third one down in this part of my hand. You got a lot of weight there! . . . All right, then you pull the string, pick up four more—swish! You're done; two moves. Three moves after you picked up the ball. So before the ball gets to the end I got the pins sitting on the deck again, waiting for another ball. And I'd do another alley—I'd double. One, two, swish, swish. I'd get madder than hell if they'd fuck me up and throw before I was ready. I'd set at least three leagues every night, sometimes four. That's thirty lines a week . . ."

After a short silence, I said, "I was thinking about blowing the fifteen hundred that we were talking about last night—"

"—Fifteen hundred, that's nothing," Carl interrupted. "You probably got acquaintances that spend more than that on foolishness! I don't care if I'm broke today and get busted tomorrow—I just don't care."

"I guess what I'm saying is that money ought to bring you at least a good time . . ."

"I'm not squawking about it," Carl said, "you brought it up."

"Well, you were a little depressed about it when I met you," I replied.

"Why sure! And you know why, don't you? 'Cause I figured—why the hell did I use the money for this. I could have bought a good car, or I could have done this, or . . . I'm second guessing myself, see. And I'm feeling sorry for myself. Now, that's the wrong thing to do!"

"But we're going to make three or four hundred dollars here. What are you going to do with that?"

Carl replied quickly: "Put it in my hip pocket."

"Then what are you going to do?"

"I'm going to move right to the next job. You know what's comin' up, don't you?"

"Winter?"

"Snowbanks; damn right!"

"So you aren't going to drink now?" I asked.

"No—no. I'll probably go up and see my mother. But I won't look like this when I go there."

"In other words, you're telling me you drink for vacations."

"On vacations. I take about two a year."

"Two a year. Right. I guess I caught you coming down from one back there in Minneapolis, eh?" Carl chuckled, and I said: "You were the sorriest looking sonofabitch when I met you—"

"—Beard down to here," Carl interrupted, "dirty . . ."

"You looked like some old derelict, sitting in the drizzle protecting your boxcar . . .

"If you didn't spend money drinking . . . ," I began to ask, but Carl interrupted.

"What would I do with it? I don't know. You tell me, you've got all the questions, you tell me the answers."

"Look, Carl," I said, "people don't have any trouble buying things—you're supposed to buy things, go into debt . . ."

"I did that one time," he said, "just one time in my life. When I came out of the service—and this was my first enlistment, I bought a Grand Page Straight-Eight. That car was a block long and it went like a sonofabitch. It'd do a hundred-fifty."

"Sure."

"It will! Anyway, it don't matter. But it was used for whiskey runs—I run whiskey with it myself. So I bought it through the finance company. I had to go to work so I worked for my brother. Now, my brother's cheap. He thinks you should work for nothin'. You end up working for him for room and board, and that's it. So the finance company starts getting on me to pay for the car. So I go to work somewhere else. And I'm payin' . . . Finally I got the principal paid off. Then I got the interest left, see. So I paid until I thought it was fair, and then said: 'Fuck you!' "

"Till *you* thought it was fair?"

"That's what I did and I got away with it. I says, 'You take me to the judge, if you want to—I'll tell him what I told you. I paid fair interest and I ain't payin' no more. And then the goddamn timing-chain went out and ruined the engine—I lost the car anyway!"

"So what's the lesson?" I asked.

"Never borrow money. Not from a finance company, not from a bank. Not from any institution—I'll borrow from a friend—a personal loan, where it isn't going to cost me an arm and a leg.

"I've watched my brother spend his whole life getting out of debt," he continued, "and now he's an old man. So who in the hell is going to get it? 'Course he's got kids, his children will get it. But he's an old man before his time . . .

"Yeah, I don't think much of these earthly possessions, to tell the truth," Carl continued. "I don't believe in anything this earth has got. Not a thing. I came into this world naked, and I'm going to leave it naked. People lose their sense of values when they start cravin' all those things, and the next thing they know it's their neighbor's wife. That ain't no good—no way!"

"But you talked about something that I understand, that I want too, which is a cabin and a piece of land . . ."

"That's all I want," Carl said.

"Then why don't you buy it?"

"I'm not old enough yet. I already told you that."

"You could buy it and keep it—there wouldn't be anything wrong with that."

He didn't answer my question. These probably weren't any answers. He told me about a cabin around Troy, Montana, that he could get for five hundred dollars, and when I said that if that was what they cost, I'd buy one next to his . . . he replied: "That's what I'm trying to get away from—*neighbors* . . .

119

"When I get older that's what I'll like. I'm changing as I get older. You seen what happened when that guy started bothering you, I jumped right down his neck. And if you'd a tried to give him something—I'd'a grabbed it and threw it in the dirt. Because I was mad. We had nothing and there he is, drinking a bottle of wine and then coming bumming. I watched that bum bummin' those hippie kids in that flower car of theirs—that van. And that pissed me! He's in there, drunk and filthy, begging. Why, all those people think we're all like that!

"I know," Carl continued, "those hippie kids, they're good-hearted. Some of them anyway. But they ain't doin' no good for anybody buying them wine. I don't go for that shit—let them dry out when they run out of money. People gotta take care of themselves on the road—*I* do.

"I treat other people like I want to be treated," he continued, "and it pisses me that they don't do back. I told you that—they always use me. Somebody's always used me. Right back to when I was a kid. That's the story of my life."

"But you've called yourself a 'freeman.' "

"I did, and I am. I can leave here tonight—it's that simple. I ain't tied to nothin', and you ought to know that by now."

"It's an old issue, Carl. It's good not to be beholden to anybody, but maybe sometimes you leave too easily."

"That's because you don't understand. We get angry too easily, but we're a different breed. Did you ever read about the people that explored? Like Lewis and Clark? The mountain men, that's what I think this tramp is about. We're a generation too late. If you gave us a long-rifle, a pair of buckskins and a pair of moccasins a hundred, or, a hundred fifty years ago, we'd be right at home. Not the heroes, don't get me wrong. Just the explorers. Go out by ourself all winter long, live with a squaw maybe, and trap and hunt. Then we'd be in our element. Because we can make do and make things on our own."

"I can see that's true by the way you acted on our trip. You came up with things I never would have found or known how to use," I said. "You knew what you were doin'."

"And we ain't one bit afraid of work."

"That's true, that's clear to me . . . Yes, I thought that it was very

120

interesting, those days waiting for the job. The tramps got by. The others worked on a bottle and let themselves go to hell."

Carl said that the black men around were tramps no less than anybody else. The fact that they drank made no difference. "You know that a colored man will drink—that's part of his nature," Carl said, and when I disagreed, he said: "Offer them a drink and see what happens!" He said that they were all probably working at the Hiland Orchard, where the trees were grown on steep hillsides and the picking was hard. They worked harder and made less money. I asked Carl if that meant that he respected them because they were good workers and he said: "Sure, I respect them. But I still don't like them."

15

We worked harder and harder. The apples ripened quickly and soon the work became routine. We worked long hours and while we both improved, Carl was still picking nearly a third more than I was. We had little time in the evenings and Carl did not encourage the kinds of conversations we had had until one day when the rain kept us in the cabin. We had begun work as usual and when rain began falling I had returned to the cabin. Carl did not return and I was given the job of bringing him home as the boss did not want the pickers climbing up and down ladders when they were wet. Carl was skirting a tree, picking the apples around the base, and he replied that he was smart enough to stay off the ladder. Only when I told him that the boss himself had told me to go out and bring him in did he follow me back to the cabin.

We drank coffee to warm up in the chill of the cabin. There was little to do and I commented that as before, I found sitting around the most difficult part of the life. Carl answered with a story of how he had spent the winter before last with a tramp named Will Louie. He and his buddy had built a cabin as large as ours out of packing crates and cardboard, and Louie had made a stove out of a ten-gallon can. It was near a peach orchard on the banks of the Yuba River in California. Carl would cut wood from dead peach trees piled near the orchard while his companion sharpened scissors and saws for liquor money. Their food came from stamps.

"If you're bored now," Carl said, "try a winter like that!"

I asked him if that was what his retirement would be like.

"No, no," he answered, "that's just fucking around. When I retire I'm going to have something coming in. Most of these tramps think they're making out giving the wrong social security number every job they get—well, they're going to get caught up with—there ain't going to be no money when they need it! They'll go right to the mission; that'll be the only way for them. Or, if they lied off and on they'll get about twenty-three, or twenty-five dollars a month. But if you work since social security started, like *I* did, and every job I git, I insist they take social security out—all right, I got quite a bit paid in."

We dawdled about the cabin for a few minutes, walking to the door to watch the rain beat furiously against the trees, and finally I asked him just what he did on a binge that cost fifteen hundred dollars.

He explained it to me patiently: "To begin with," he said, "I get cleaned up. No, I don't get fancy clothes, just clean clothes, like my grays, or my khakis . . . You don't have to dress up to spend money, just be clean . . .

"The last time I stayed in the Coeur d' Alene Hotel in Spokane. One of the better hotels, well, it used to be, although it ain't no more.

"I stayed drunk for a month, but it's maybe not what you'd call drunk, it's more like *continual drinking*. A man can only get so drunk—after that he passes out . . .

"All right, so when you wake up you're going to have to take a drink if you want to feel better, or else you'll have to cut it out altogether. It takes so many drinks to start feeling good, and then you start spacing your drinks. You know—just to keep yourself aglow. You don't drink just boom-boom-boom like some guys do—no, no!"

I said: "I've always suffered through my hangovers and not started over again."

"So you're a periodic drunk! . . . That's what you are—you're a periodic drunk. You might call it a 'social drinker' but that ain't exactly accurate. Now, can you do this: get drunk, stop, start and then space your drinking like I do? I keep good and high so I won't feel the effects afterward. It takes a couple of quarts a day. At least

122

two a day—that's about three in twenty-four hours. That's about twenty or twenty-five dollars a day for the booze. Then you figure twenty for your room, or fifteen, depending on where you're at. And then you're going to eat a good steak dinner at night. You're going to order it even if you don't eat it. And you're going to go in about ten in the morning and eat your breakfast, even if you don't eat two bites, you're still going to pay, and a big restaurant costs like hell. Then, of course, you're going to have a shoe-shine. You got to have a shave at the barber shop, you know—that's about five bucks . . . get the trim, too, you know, the works . . .

"And then you sit down in the lobby, and glance through the paper like everything's okay, but what you're really waiting for is that lounge to open up so you can have a drink. You got it up in your room but you'd rather drink in that lounge. And then there's your tips, too. You gotta tip—if you don't, you don't get service at all. It's nothing to me to throw a half a buck tip to the waitress. Drinks a dollar and a quarter, a dollar and a half—throw her a half buck—it all adds up!"

"Why do you quit that kind of a drunk? Do you drink until you're broke?"

"I get bored! I get bored with it! What the hell, I ain't doin' nothin', I'm just sittin'."

"I would think it would get boring. When I think of spending time drinking I think of going out with people I like and drinking."

Carl snorted: "You're just like some of us—you can't find your friends but in barrooms. But like you said, where else are you going to meet your buddies? Are you going to meet them in church? You can't talk like we are in church. You going to meet them in a poolroom? There ain't no more good poolrooms. Where else is there to meet? You tell me of someplace else there is to meet."

"Well, if you have a house, if you have a place . . ."

"*If* you got a house. We ain't got houses. We got a bedroll. So we get together aroung a jungle, a fire, and bullshit. And then if we meet each other in a tavern we bullshit, but then we drink too!"

"Then are the lives of the men in the jungles there in Pateros the same as yours? Would they agree with all this?"

Carl answered slowly: "Well, somewhat. They might not follow the same area, or they might drink a different liquor . . . some of them I won't trust. Anybody that's got that you-all . . . they're too much light-fingered. Where do you think my good radio disappeared to? That's where it's at—Delores and Dusty are 'you-alls.' "

"But after a man has been on the road for twenty years, how could it matter where he came from?"

"It does matter. That's ingrained, you know. And I'll tell you something, once a thief, always a thief. And that's no lie. Once a murderer, always a murderer."

"No rehabilitation?"

"Damn right. And don't you ever forget it, either. They'll never change, not in my book."

Carl walked over to the door to watch the rain. After a few minutes he said: "We can be glad we got this cabin. How would you like to be camping in the weeds today?"

After a few minutes, I asked: "What if at the end of the harvest, if you were traveling through Pateros and met four or five of the men we were jungling with—would you drink with them? Would you go into a bar for one night and drink with them for one night?"

"If they're broke," Carl said, "I'll give them enough for a jug. I won't drink. I can have five or six hundred dollars in my pocket and I won't drink. It don't matter to *me*! I'll tell them right now—I'll buy them a drink but I won't drink with them."

"But you said that that is where you meet your buddies, in the barroom . . ."

"They're not my buddies," Carl said, "they're just acquaintances. My buddies—I got very, very few. And, I can count my friends on one hand. Now, you're my buddy, you're not my friend—yet. Friends I make once, and that's all. I learned that in the army, after a while you don't make them because it hurts too much to lose them—army taught me that."

He paused, then continued, "Friendship is hard to get. You know, people use that word loosely. Very loosely. What they should say is buddy, or pal, or something like that—but a real friend is damn hard to find. Because a real friend is just like yourself. You'd do anything for yourself; all right, you'd also do that for a friend. If your friend needs it, he takes it even if it means *you* go without. He's your friend. But if it's a buddy, I won't do that. I'll share with a buddy, you know, equal shares—fine. But a friend, I'll go out of my way to help. I'll look him up. That's different. There's a hell of a big difference there . . . No, my buddies, I can take them or leave them. Like these guys in the jungle? If I ever see them again: 'How you doin', where you been,' . . . all that. Same with the tramps in this orchard. 'How was the harvest, how much did you make? Who'd you see? Did you see so and so?' Like we did every night in the jungle. But to go drink with them in a tavern? No, no. Even if I see them in a tavern, if I don't want to drink with them, I won't. If I'm drinkin' by myself, I'll ignore them. I'll say hello, buy them a drink, but then I'll turn my back."

"So it's not the kind of situation where you'll go in for an evening of sociable drinking."

"With those kind of people?" Carl asked, "No thanks!"

"But they're tramps!"

"Sure they're tramps," Carl answered, "but they're not drinking companions. You know those people change—they're like Dr. Jekel and Mr. Hyde. They take two drinks, and man, they want to fight. They might fight you! They're wet-brains, those people."

I asked him: "How do you change when you drink?"

"I just talk more," he replied. "And I remember more. I get a clearer mind. But then when I get off it my mind gets befuddled. You ever been on this . . . In the army they gave it to us to keep awake."

"Speed."

"I guess maybe. Benzedrine—they had those little tablets. But that wasn't strong enough. Do you know those inhalers? We used to chew those. It'd get you higher than a kite. And you want to see a guy that can talk? It makes you mind real sharp . . . you can remember . . . but when you get off it . . . bad."

"Yeah," I said, "a lot of people begin on heroin trying to make the end of a speed trip easier to get through. After five or six days on speed, coming down is bad. Heroin smoothes that out."

"I've never taken it like that," Carl said. "Anyway, it can't be the same stuff. They gave it to us in the army."

"It's the same stuff. Speed. Goes by many different names. Truck drivers are the biggest bunch of speed freaks in the country."

"But they used to give us that in the *army*," Carl repeated.

"Were you in the front lines?" I said, "I've heard that they gave it to the men who were in the front lines."

125

"I was. In the islands. They gave it to us to keep us awake. Christ, we'd be up there for ten, fifteen days at a crack. They didn't have nobody to relieve us. Guadalcanal, Iwo Jima . . . I'm a combat veteran, you know."

"You were on those beaches?"

"Why certainly. What do you think I'm talking about? How many times do you think we lost Henderson Field?

"And Guadalcanal . . . We lost it seven or eight times. Lose it one day, take it back the next."

"You must have seen a lot fall . . ."

"That's what I told you," Carl said, "you make friends only once! You never make a friend again. When those guys used to come as replacements in the front lines—nobody would talk to them. And they couldn't understand it. But they learned after a while. When they saw their own buddies fall, they learned."

"You mean you were on the front lines that landed on the beaches?"

"Hell, yes, what do you think? LST's . . ."

"The front of that boat dropped open and you charged that beach against that . . ."

". . . fire," Carl interrupted.

"Jesus Christ."

"Packsack on my back . . ."

"I always wondered," I said, "what would make a man jump out of that boat, people shooting like crazy. I'm sure *I* wouldn't do it."

"Yes, you would," Carl answered. "Do you know why? You don't want your buddies to think you're yellow. You're shittin' in your pants, but you go. Yeah, we'd fight and fight for a piece of coral, bombard the shit out of it, and after we'd capture it they'd be nothing left of it anyway!

"I drank," he said, "like any soldier did. Three-two beer . . . that's where I got this . . . ," he showed a faded tattoo on his arm. "The first time I ever drank in my life I was nineteen years old. G.I. party in the barracks, '43. I drank about three cans of three-two beer and I'm drunk! Next morning I wake up with a sore arm. Huh? Tatooed!" He laughed at himself, "I went home, saw my mother, oh, Christ!"

He was in a fairly bad mood because one of his few remaining teeth was loose. He pushed and pulled on it, and then said: "Yeah, this mess is due to the army too. When I went in everything was above boards. They're going to take good care of me—fine, wonderful. So they put twenty-three temporary fillings into my teeth and sent me overseas. Six months later they all dropped out. What am I going to do? There ain't no dentists over there. Well, my teeth went to hell. They been dropping out, and everything else, since. And if you let them go for a year and a half or something like that—you're too late. It'd cost me a fortune to get them fixed. So I pulled them and the government says it's not service-related. They conveniently lost the dental charts."

I thought about what we'd been talking about, then said: "Do you have everything you want?"

"He-ell no!" Carl replied. Then he thought for a moment: "I do now; I'm still alive, I got a job, a place to sleep. What more? . . . I got money coming, if I want to leave I can leave . . ."

I answered: "Maybe I want too much stuff."

"Sure," Carl was quick to agree, "you know what you want, don't you? You want to keep up with the Joneses."

"No, no, that just isn't true! I want things like . . ."

"You want material things, don't you."

"I don't think I do but what you say might be truer than I'd care to admit. But there is the thing of love and friendship . . . I still harbor the idea that I might have a family, children, all that. My family gets along well, and I think that it would be good to have something like that myself."

"All of that is natural," Carl said, surprising me. "It's human nature. But is that what you're looking for now?" When I didn't answer, Carl said, "Or are you trying to find yourself?" I mumbled something and Carl repeated: "Are you trying to find a family, or are you trying to find yourself?"

"I'm trying to find myself," I answered, and Carl replied: "Well, that's more like it! Now you're honest. There's something that brought you here, just like there's something that brought me, isn't there? You're not so different than me, then, are you?"

"I don't think I am," I said. "I think that there are a lot of things about me that I wish were more like you."

"And there are things that you know you are not going to be like; ways that are no good."

I had a hard time answering the tramp. I told him I thought he had a lot of the world pretty well figured out. Carl surprised me by saying: "Those others are living good in a way . . . They can put their name on the line and get all those things, and I can't. 'Course I'm glad of it! I can't even get foodstamps unless I lie, and I ain't going to lie to get them. I won't go out and live like those people—they come off the job and they spend their money for liquor—then they go right to the foodstamp people. 'Have you worked in the last three months?' 'Nooo, nooo.' They sign their name and it's notarized! They could get it for perjury!

"Or you can go into an employment office and see the same thing, only in a different way. They lie about the work they've done in order to get unemployment payments. Perjury . . . lying under oath . . . six of one, half dozen of another. Something I can't do," his voice was rising, "you know, I'd rather be with a thief than a liar. A thief, I know what he's going to do. A liar, I never know. A thief can hurt you financially, but a liar can hurt you morally. They can hurt your reputation and everything about you."

Carl asked me what I was going to do when the harvest was over. When I told him I was going back to school, he asked me what I was going to do when it was finished. I said I wanted to be a teacher and a writer. "Are you going to write about this?" he asked. I told him I was, as I had earlier in out trip, and I said he was a more important teacher than most I'd had.

He said he had more common sense than most intellectual people had knowledge. "I live the facts," he said. "The facts of my life are the same facts of your so-called scientific experiments. You can't dispute the facts of my life!"

He mellowed some, and added, "I'm older, too. You'll gain that in time."

"But what you tell me, and what we experience, is the facts," I said.

"Don't be fooled," Carl replied, "some of it's hogwash.

"You know, I found something out today"; Carl changed the topic. "You ought to have seen those women look at you. You know why? Because you're polite to them. And they came up and told me, 'Hey, he's a nice kid' . . . I even heard you once, talking to one of those women that drives the tractors. You were polite to them. You don't yell, or scream like the rest of us. That's the kind they are used to—they're not used to your kind of person."

"I was disagreeing with them. I told them I thought they ought to hang Nixon by his fucking balls."

"So, that's your choice. But that makes you different, the way you talk. That one was standing there when you came over to bring me the water. She was standing there and you said something to her. I forget what it was, I didn't pay no attention. I think you said, 'ma'am' or something, and she looked at you so funny. She ain't used to that. It's usually, 'Hey, you' or something like that. They'll respect you for it, because those women are older than you think. That one today happened to be the owner's wife, and she said later: 'He's a pretty nice guy.' And you don't think that makes a difference?

"But like I said, that kind of nice ain't found on the road. You learn too fast that it will only get you in trouble."

"It's not as though I don't think about it," I said. "That first night in the boxcar I was going to sleep next to the door, and I was thinking—this is really stupid! That old guy doesn't have much gear . . ."

"What am I going to do," Carl interrupted, "steal it and jump out at fifty miles an hour?"

"All I am saying is that I didn't know you from nobody. You looked rough. Rough, I was layin' next to the fuckin' door.

"So I was laying there thinking, everybody tells me I'm too trusting, and here's one of those times people warn me about! But I was sleepy. A little nervous, but mostly sleepy. So I went to sleep. And when I woke up you were still there, and my gear was still there."

"It'll hurt you eventually," Carl said, "you got off this time, but it'll catch up. You got to be more wary, but it don't hurt to have some fucking manners. Did you see that one guy at the employment trailer?" he asked. "He went right out in back and took a leak, with a woman standing right there . . . He knew that woman could see him. I felt about that high," Carl continued, measuring an inch with his fingers. "If I could have hid under that ground, I would have—and did you notice all the others? They just turned their heads. They wouldn't look at him."

I showed my surprise.

"It embarrassed them," Carl Said, "that woman was classifying all of us by his action. And it embarrassed all of us. But we wouldn't say nothing, it was too late! But that guy dropped a notch right there."

129

"That's something I've noticed that I guess I found a little surprising. The tramp stays out of sight because he doesn't want to be treated like a bum. Angler Joe there wouldn't hitchhike to that orchard—he walked the seventeen miles along a railroad track because he didn't want all those cars going by him, I suppose honking, or making faces. Still, he might have got a ride."

"That's right," Carl agreed, "he'd rather walk along the tracks, where it's hard to walk. Well, I'm the same way. I won't walk down that road. I've had it happen to me—people yell at you, throw things at you. And it ain't just along the road. We were lucky we didn't get "rocked" coming over. The kids are back in school. Well, if they hadn't been in school—we'd have had to watch it the whole trip. I was going to warn you—you're like all newcomers, you like to stand in that doorway and let the people see you like you're a hot shit. You've got to watch it, or you're going to get it. It's the easiest way to put your eyes out. Just like that guy, One-Eyed Jack, we talked to. Same thing."

"I know," I said. "Last year when I was riding every tramp I talked to was scared about getting hit with a rock. They weren't afraid of getting rolled, or busted by the bull, they were afraid of getting hit by a rock thrown by a kid."

"We got a few, you know," Carl said, "That first night coming out of Helena. Just after the sun set that first night. Two kids on a motorbike. Right away they got scared, then they took off. They think it's smart, but if you ever got hit with one of them—it'd tear your head off! You can't see it coming, that's the the worst part . . .

"If I would have expected it I'd'a told you—you stay away from those doors. Especially goin' through town. And any time you see kids—right away, get out of the way. Duck. Don't let them see you! And it's not just kids, it's grown people, too. A lot of the tramps carry 'nigger shooters,' that's a slingshot. You don't aim for them; you aim for their feet. It'll put some fire in their ass—teach them a lesson pretty quick. Just draw it back, you don't have to have a rock in it. If you want to see those kids split!" Carl laughed in spite of himself. "Or you just throw with your forearm. They'll duck, they'll run like hell. They know that if they get hit it'll kill them. That's the speed of the train plus the speed of the rock—man, it's just like a bullet.

"They stand up on the bridges," Carl continued, "I'll never ride a

130

gondola on the outside! And there used to be high banks through Spokane. The old bridge went along a residential section and the kids would stand up there and throw rocks at you. If they get caught they get punished with a slap on the wrist. They might knock somebody's eye out, or raise havoc with the new cars that go by. Break windows in the caboose. But they caught some kids—I seen them—and all they did was slap them on the wrist and send them home."

We rambled on about one thing after another. Carl was talking about how "John Q. Public" was always getting screwed but then he said the whole country was going to hell because everybody had lost their morals. He told me about a Jules Verne story he'd read where a man invented a time machine and went into the future until he found a utopia. The traveler returned to his society and then traveled back to the utopia with certain books: "He found his utopia and he was going to change it," Carl said. Every society fell apart, he said, because of some built-in tendency man had to screw himself up. "That's a lot of what makes us tramps," he said, "we realize that 'getting ahead' is just a lot of bullshit." Then he looked at me to catch my attention: "I've noticed you change—you've learned that you can make it on the road. Now, if something overloads, it'll always be in the back of your mind—you might find this *too* attractive, but maybe it will be a different version. You don't have to ride freights to be a tramp, you know . . . You got to remember, it ain't what you got, it's how you live. Like those people we watched going along the highway in their big fancy trailers. Would you like to live like that? They're afraid to sleep on the ground. They couldn't do what we've been doing! They'd turn up their noses up at the perfectly good food we've been eating and they got to cover their heads up. They live for those things and they can't live without them. But it wears on you, too. This ain't like me. You remember in the boxcar I would be on my feet every time we even slowed down. Well, this morning the alarm woke me and that's the first time in so goddamn long . . . I forgot when! And you're sleeping there. That's the first time that that happened since I can remember. I'm not used to this. I've known guys for years that if they sleep in the same room with me, I'm nervous as a cat. I'm real nervous. You call it energy—I just call it nerves."

We ate lunch and sat around the cabin. There was absolutely nothing to do; nowhere to go. We were both getting a little cabin fever

131

and when the rain slowed up that afternoon I took a walk down through the orchard to the river. Carl didn't say anything when I returned but looked at me like I was crazy for walking around getting wet. We fixed dinner and ate in silence, and finally, when dinner was finished he asked me about my trip to India and when I started describing the way the people lived there, he said: "You take the American culture—our way of life—and give it to the savage. What do you do? You make him just as unhappy as we are. They were getting along fine, in their own primitive way. Wonderful. No fighting, maybe just a little in-fighting, but everyone had enough to eat. Of course, their death rate was higher than ours and they weren't as clean . . . but they were happy. So we went in and we brought them our diseases, and we corrupted them with our trinkets, so they would want all that shit they don't need. Greed, violence . . . every foreign place we've touched." I said modern countries went to foreign countries to find cheap labor and he interrupted me: "We got it right here in Washington. What do you think we are? Cheap labor, that's what. Here when they need us; out when they're finished."

The next day it rained more and I had to get out of the cabin. I hitched into town but the bars were too depressing to stay in for long. I found a store with used paperbacks and bought a handful. I hitched back to the orchard feeling better but Carl was his old silent self. He read one of the books, Miller's *View from the Bridge*, and when I asked him what he thought about it he said: "Bunch of fucking dagos killing each other over a woman. I don't see what's so good about that!"

The next day was clear and we went back to work. The goldens were soon finished and we started on the reds. They were bruised less easily and the trees were loaded. We were making good money, but it didn't seem to mean anything to Carl. He'd start before dawn, and work long after everybody had quit. He was deteriorating physically—his hands cracked and bled and he wheezed and spat all the time but still smoked a couple of packs a day. His left hand was numb all the time and he kept getting dizzy and losing his balance. He'd sit up in bed and yell out as charley horses tied his leg muscles in knots, but he never let up. I didn't know what it was all for, and if he knew, he wasn't telling.

Wenatchee sunrise

horseshoe bend between Helena and Missoula on the Great
Northern bull local

northern Montana

jungle; Wenatchee

jungle; Wenatchee

waiting for the harvest; northern Washington

footprints in the jungle

westbound near Walla Walla

Okanogan River; apple knockers, jackrollers and riffraff

harvest jungle

". . . when / please"

eastbound near Klamath Falls

coming down from a three-week drunk

harvester; northern Washington orchard

orchard cabin

waiting for a train; Seattle

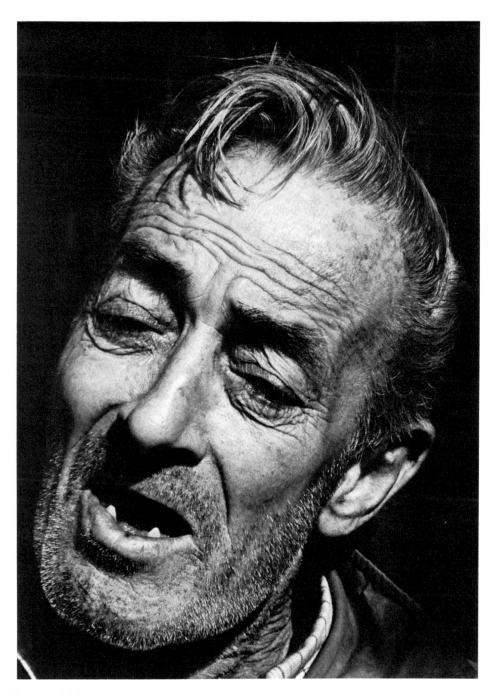

Boston skid row

Havre, Montana

Kalispell, Montana

eastbound on the Minnesota / North Dakota border

16

As the tramp kept more and more to himself I began to make plans to head east. Our relationship had gone a full circle and we lived in sullen isolation from each other. I was saddened by the change; I learned I'd invested more than I should.

I noticed other changes in my attitudes. I felt psychologically hardened and I felt that I took my own future less for granted. My trip had opened odd possibilities, some that were disconcerting. It would be easy to stay on the road and I considered extending my trip by a month; maybe two, three or four. As the weather turned colder, talk was of oranges in Florida, lemons in California. I was pushed and pulled by the same forces that affected the others and I knew that if there was a scheme, there would be somebody to share it with. Perhaps most important, I'd begun to sense the balance between my vulnerability and my ability to survive. I'd learned that there would be work if I steeled myself once again to the road; what was most unsettling was the threat of loss of future, the immersion in the present that was the tramp life.

I began spending my evenings with other tramps in the orchard. A rubber tramp named Roy lived in a cabin by ours and I fell into the habit of stopping by after dinner for a few shots of whiskey. One night four of us were sitting around drinking out of old jelly jars when Roy told us about two years before when he'd been in Wenatchee and had seen five policemen marching thirty tramps down to the freight yard: "I watched the cops march them over to a freight that was made up—nobody asked where it was going, they knew that all that mattered was it was going out of town. And those cops stood there until that freight highballed out of there—nobody was getting out the other side!"

Another tramp, Jack, said: "I don't think they do that much no more. Last year a boy fell off one and cut his legs off and sued the hell out of the railroad, so I don't think they do that much anymore."

Rob answered: "That may be, but this time I saw it with my own eyes, thirty men in double-file being marched through town to the freight yard . . . Never seen anything like it before!"

I asked him if he still rode now and then and he laughed when he answered: "That's for you kids. I got my Ford automobile out there!" (The starter was lying in pieces on the floor of his cabin, however.) "The last time I rode? Well, let's see . . . Last trip I took was five years ago. We were down in Portland—God, them yards is hot! They don't let you near them! . . . It was around Christmas. On Christmas in the mission they had a hell of a nice meal for us—fruit on the tables, tablecloths—yeah, it was really nice. My buddy and I were sick of looking at the goddarn rain and I said: 'Hell, let's go down to California and pick those lemons.' 'I'm with you, buddy.' So we went to the next town by way of our thumbs, but we couldn't get near those yards. We had to grab the freight on the run goin' down south. We pretty near froze to death and I'm not kidding. I had a sleeping bag and we had plenty of cardboard but riding over that hump into Klamath Falls is cold! We got down to Redland and started looking for a freight into L.A. Do you know we waited five days, five miserable, cold, raining—the goddamn rain did not stop once—looking for an empty into L.A.? Every time a freight would make up we'd walk the length of it looking for an empty. Get soaking wet but never find an empty. We was going to ride a piggyback, but hell in that cold and rain I'd last about five miles. We were camped in an empty on a siding and our food was running low. Finally, I told my buddy: 'Fuck those lemons, I'm going back to Portland!' 'I'm with you, buddy!' So we grabbed the last train north, prid'near froze my ass off going over that hump again and came highballing into Portland. You know that yard is red-hot so we were going to jump him outside the yards, out by that golf course. You know the golf course, Jack?"

"Yep, I sure do," the other tramp answered.

"So we're moving about fifteen miles an hour through the golf course and neither one of us had the guts to jump. So we sailed right into the yards, right past the bull in his shack. See, in Portland the bulls got their own shacks, right out there by the end of the yard and if they grab you, it's thirty days, no questions asked, those dicks are bastards. He sees us and is yellin': 'You boys stay right there in that boxcar'—he grabs the ladder on the next car. My buddy and I looked at each other and all of a sudden we weren't afraid no more about jumpin', so out the other side we went and we ran all the damn way out of that yard! And that was the last ride I took."

I decided to leave on a Saturday morning, late in the harvest. I'd become friends with the foreman, who offered to take me around the towns for an evening. I went with him that night through bar after bar where watered bourbon cost thirty-five cents and Lucky Lager chasers a dime. The bars were full of harvest money but they were depressing; surprisingly quiet and dismal. By midnight most of the men were passed out in booths or stumbling drunk and incoherent. I recognized a man we'd jungled with waiting for the harvest and I approached him as I'd approach an old friend, but there was no sign of recognition as he mumbled drunkenly, "Do you have a quarter for a drink . . ."

There was not one woman in any of the bars until late in the night when a fat woman with stringy hair circled the bar, propositioning everyone openly. She finally led an old man out the door where there would be, said the foreman, someone waiting to roll him.

We were about to head back when my companion pointed through the murk: "See over there—that's a jackroller. He ain't been drinking, but he's pretending to be drunk."

A tramp started making trouble and the bartender, a man with fists the size of hams, threw him matter-of-factly through the door into the street. Thirty seconds later the jackroller followed. When he walked by I recognized him—it as the same man Carl and I had ridden up with from Wenatchee. "Watch him," Carl had warned, "he's here to pick the pickers!" The jackroller came back alone in a few minutes, and then, just before the bar closed he led another tramp outside, this one so drunk he could barely stand. It was grim reality, but there was nothing to do. If the cops got involved, they'd lose their money on their way to the drunk tank instead of the gutter.

I packed the next morning before breakfast but Carl didn't ask what I was up to. I told him I was leaving, and he shrugged and said simply that if I rode the freights this time of year I'd be a fool. He finished his breakfast, washed out his pie tin, picked his sack off the wall and walked out the door without saying goodbye. We'd been together for more than a month.

I picked up my check and talked for a few minutes with the owner. I was particularly interested in how he saw the men he hired; what vision came from the vantage point he occupied. He said: "What I know about each one of them you could put in a nutshell. They never talk to an outsider and they don't like a lot of questions. They work for a person like me because they can be their own boss. They start in the morning and work as long as they want. As long as they pick clean fruit there are very few dealings between us—not that I wish it was that way—I'd really like to know what they think of this operation. But they're loners, and I've found that if I do my part—supply a good, clean cabin, offer rides to town for groceries, and only ride herd when a picker is bruising the fruit or screwing up the trees—the system works the best . . .

"There's talk of an automatic picker. If such a machine comes into use I'll still need workers, but I can tell you it won't be the tramp, what they call the 'apple knocker.' Don't get me wrong—I'd like to have the tramp because they work damn hard. But if I had a machine picking in the orchard, there'd have to be organization—regular hours, work crews and everybody working to the pace of the picker. The tramp'd never do that—not in a million years. They're too independent and they live their life by whims. They have to be able to come and go whenever they please, and work without someone looking over their shoulder."

His wife drove me to the nearest town where I ate a second breakfast and cashed my check, then I hitched southeast toward Spokane. The rides were easy that day and I was in the city early in the afternoon. I thought maybe I'd take the bus back to Minnesota, but my ride took me by the Burlington Northern yards and there I saw what I thought to be the east-bound hotshot sitting with its power on the main line. I left my ride and ran across the yard as the train started idling ahead. The engineer yelled an obscenity down at me and he tried to kick the train up to speed so I would miss my ride. A line of piggybacks rolled by, and while I did not relish the thought of an outside ride I threw my gear on board and swung up.

We were soon in the flatlands on the west side of the Rockies. We crossed into Idaho heading northeast—across a railroad bridge over the Pend Oreille Lake at Sandpoint—and then into the Rocky Mountain foothills along the Kootenai River. I was hungry as I had no supplies but I was more worried about the cold which by late afternoon was already becoming severe.

The train highballed into Montana, the seven units pulling the mile-long freight seventy miles an hour. When the sun dipped below

136

the horizon I put my other set of clothes over the jeans I wore. Just as it was getting dark the train whistle-stopped in Whitefish.

Two men with no gear came running down the train and when they saw me and jumped onto my car I thought I might well be in for more than I could handle. I told them there were twenty piggybacks on the train and that I was riding that one alone. The larger man pulled a knife and his buddy started circling, walking crab-like under the truck trailer, behind me. In my fear something snapped, and when I pulled my Buck knife and started screaming at them to get the fuck off my car, they backed off, perhaps bluffing themselves, or preferring easier game. The train pulled out and I could see them further down— looking for a place to ride. My heart was beating wildly.

It was the worst of nights. I kept thinking the jackrollers had jumped further down and that they'd somehow cross the couplings to get me again. I lay up against the wheels of the truck trailer in the full blast of the wind. I turned from side to side, away from the intense, biting cold, and passed fitfully into sleep for a minute or two before I would start awake, sure that I had heard an incongruous sound amidst the pounding of the open ride. I would grab my flashlight and shine it around the car, looking for intruders who never came. The beam of light played through the metal superstructure of the flatcar and truck trailer, startling me when it shone off a bright surface or when it illuminated a hidden feature of the landscape just over the edge of the car. The night was long and cold and eerie, until I finally detected a grayish shade in the eastern sky and I knew I was only a few hours from Havre. Just as the sun rose across the horizon the train rolled to a stop.

Brakemen checking the journals were surprised to see an outside rider. I was mumbling incoherently about never, never again riding their freights and they stood back laughing: "What's wrong, tramping too tough for you? Didn't you like that eighteen-degree weather in the mountains last night?" But I was already off the train and hiking toward town. I entered the first place I found for breakfast, but sat in the corner ashamed of my rail windblown dirt. The waitress served me a steak and egg breakfast after she saw my money; then I lounged around town until I was hungry enough for another meal. I felt like Carl the tramp starting on a binge. I had money in my pocket and I didn't care what I spent it on. I bought a new set of clothes and I knew that my tramping was finished. I'd had the idea that I might ride that freight the rest of the way back to Minnesota but the Amtrak looked too good to be let out of the yards alone. I rode that passenger train back to Minnesota, eating rare beef and sipping brandy in the diner car, and forgetting, at least for the moment, the taste of beans.

Contexts

> In the field investigating . . . requires a relationship to your subjects as persons, and that must also include yourself as a person. For, if you objectify your interacting self, setting it "over there," apart from your observational self, and relate that part of you as an object (an operation often done in the name of "participant observation") you will severely limit your power to gain personal knowledge from your subjects. They will not be fooled and will keep their distance accordingly.
>
> The relationships we form with the subjects of our work—for whatever reasons we settle upon those relationships—control the kind of knowledge that the material we gain will yield. (Jay 1972, 379)

I came to share this view of fieldwork after several years of more limited involvement with those I studied. This can perhaps best be seen in a brief overview of the experiences that led to what I've described in this report.

My first work with homeless men was initiated by Jim Spradley, who suggested I photograph skid row life to illustrate a book he planned. I began this work in Boston after graduating from college. I became involved in a way I had not expected when I met and moved in with a black man who had been a junkie and a heroin pusher for most of his adult life. Our relationship led me to understand the photographs I was making more from the view of those in the images, and when Jesse went with me to photograph I learned how to be on the street as one does who gets his living there. Our commitment to each other and the work were interwoven; we began as well, a study of heroin addiction which we never completed. What we did complete seemed richer and more obviously correct than anything we could find in the sociological literature. The difference came, I believed, from the nature of our relationship. I began to feel that in order to learn anything really important about a group one needs to establish a bond greater than the one described as normally existing between researcher and informant. I came to this work, as well, with training in anthropology, particularly ethnoscience, an academic perspective which suggested that in general researchers know little of consequence about

139

the worlds they set out to analyze. In ethnoscience one not only learns the language of a group to ask questions which come from the researcher's analytic interest; one must also know what lies beneath questions members of a group routinely ask one another. Thus categories, or *definitions*, come to be understood as units of the world as experienced, and the relative character of nearly all definitions impressed me very much. It guided my work with Jesse and it remains at the basis of all I have done on the road.

The photographic project, the heroin study and efforts to reintegrate Jesse into mainstream society formed the cornerstones of our world for a year. Eventually, contradictions that developed between Jesse's values and his old life led him back to his life as an addict. I felt to a large degree responsible as I had had a lot to do with what had taken place. With arm-length tracks and no account of years of his life, even the most menial jobs were unavailable. After a while I suggested that he sell himself as a reformed junkie to the administrators of the local methadone program. Although neither of us believed in methadone, and in fact saw it as a sinister hoax, we believed the system could be manipulated to Jesse's advantage. In the end the pulls were too great. Street-wise people, many of whom he had known as a pusher, couldn't believe Jesse was straight and thought he had the best thing going—money and free drugs; and Jesse felt hypocritical pushing a drug considered more dangerous than heroin and one that was controlled by the state. When he went back he went back completely; arrested for pushing dope, he jumped bail and disappeared. I was crushed. I did not know where friendship had begun and where fieldwork had ended—but I felt I had failed at both. I was left with the terrible feeling that at least some of the repercussions of wanting to learn had seriously affected a life I cared very deeply about. Fieldwork carried responsibilities I had been ill prepared for.

I began graduate school that fall as a sociology student at Brandeis University. After what had happened in Jesse's life I had little energy for the skid row project; still, I decided to give the work a last try. To partially break down the barriers I'd maintained as an outsider, I would spend two weeks in midwinter with no money on Boston's skid row. The experience was to be part of a field methods class but I went, as well, to try to find my friend.

Skid row life from the inside introduced me to a new city. I avoided the bottle gangs and the panhandling that paid for the bottles, and wandered, feeling quite isolated, through police lines for chits to the mission and joined soup lines for food. We were let out of the mission at five every morning, not to be permitted back until late afternoon, and filling the hours between became the principal challenge I shared with the others. More and more the bottle and the sociability that surrounded getting and drinking it seemed reasonable. There was nothing else to do—certainly no way out of the life as I found that even I was unable to get daily labor. Getting the bottle represented a task to which one could devote one's skill and the release of the drunk with comrades provided a just reward. Beyond that I learned little and I gave up on the idea of learning in more depth. Perhaps the most honest thing to say is that it was just too depressing.

I spent periods of the next four years in the west, on freights and in jungles, in missions and harvests where the tramp (a hard drinker who sometimes spent his binges on skid rows, but was not a skid row man as I found in the east) formed his natural world. I've described one trip in detail. I would like to look more closely, however, at my relationship with Carl in terms of Robert Jay's suggestion that what we learn is deeply influenced by how we are with those we study.

Tramps buddy-up, which is to say that they get involved with each other by sharing food, supplies, time and miles, but they become involved with the understanding that in the end they make their own decisions and they will finally move on alone. Carl accepted my food because he was down and out, but he knew I was not a regular and he was suspicious of what he'd have to pay. During our first days together he realized I did not really know what to expect from him and he warned: "Some people on this road are helpless. When you start helpin' it's just like having a son . . . They don't know where it stops! You got to support them—take care of them—you got to provide the hand and I won't do that. If a fella is on this road and he can't learn—then to hell with him." Later, he added: "When you get your job, don't depend on nobody else. If you want to leave, then leave! That's it—a lot of these guys say, 'If you quit, let me know and I'll quit with you.' I say bullshit. Before you know it you'll have run out of places to work."

I understood even less, I realized very early, about relationships I observed among other tramps. I watched the elaborate exchange be-

141

tween Blackie and Carl and noted what I thought to be the wonderful generosity that existed naturally on the road. Later I learned that Blackie was a sonofabitch trying to get Carl indebted for future business. Yet later when we jungled before the harvest there were few supplies anywhere and everything a tramp had became common property. I slowly and awkwardly came to understand these events and to participate in them in a way that could be called normal by those in the life.

But even though Carl tried to make our relationship typical, it never was. At first he taught me how to make it on the road and ignored most of my questions. Something changed the chemistry between us and he stepped out of his normal role to tell me about his childhood, his parents, and his life before hitting the road. I had learned not to expect such self-revelation, and I think Carl sensed as well that they constituted transgressions of the normal tramp way. At the end he distanced himself again and made it clear that the things we had been discussing were off limits and that when it came time to leave he would be on his way alone.

My sociological eye observed all this, yet my emotional character acted on its own. In becoming committed to Carl the individual (as opposed to Carl the tramp) I offered unwanted advice and rather unconsciously set out to reform my buddy. Carl humored me—I told him he ought to put a part of his stash in the bank before he started a binge, and he said: "I do—bartender's bank!" Or, after telling me he expected to buy a cabin in Montana and I said I'd like that too, he replied: "That's what I want to get away from . . . neighbors." But finally, I began to feel a grudging respect and a partial acceptance. Just before I left he said: "I've noticed you change. You've learned that you can make it on the road—now if something overloads it'll always be in the back of your mind . . . You watch yourself—you'll be reverting back."

But as I became more like Carl in manner and behavior, and perhaps more hardened by the experiences we shared, I could not leave my other values behind. When he opened up to me I responded with friendship (a category from my life, not his). When he distanced himself I felt rebuffed, and I felt a great loss at the end of our time together. I never really learned to experience the world as a tramp and

142

I knew that unless I moved completely into that life my values would probably remain in the world of relationships and commitments.

While I have described a field method based on learning through psychological as well as physical involvement there remains the problem, basic to all fieldwork, of rigor and generality. In sociology these issues are called validity—whether what we report is true; and reliability—the concern that what we report accurately represents a class of events or types. In a fieldwork experience we usually narrow our sample to one or a few individuals happened upon in what is usually a haphazard or accidental manner—certainly not a manner which can be replicated very easily. While I acknowledge that these are serious issues, I do not believe that in and of themselves they invalidate the field methods approach. Part of my commitment to this approach lies in the belief that whatever narrowness an intensive field study necessitates, it more than makes up for in the depth it produces. My teacher and friend Everett Hughes puts it this way: "Among the methods I would recommend is the intensive, penetrating look with an imagination as lively and sociological as it can be made. One of my basic assumptions is that if one quite clearly sees something happen once, it is almost certain to have happened again and again. The burden of proof is on those who claim a thing once seen is an exception; if they look hard, they may find it everywhere, although with some interesting differences in each case" (Hughes 1971, ix). If we can assume that I have "seen clearly," that the month spent with Carl represents a typical space of time, that the conversations I have chosen to communicate represent typical exchanges, and that the effect of a nontramp in a tramp role has not influenced the reality to the point where it has been seriously distorted, still there is the question of how much we may generalize about tramp life from what we have learned about Carl.

In a later part of this report I have characterized the tramp world in part as a cycle of drinking, migrating and working. I participated in a migration and a session of work. There were extensive conversations about drinking although Carl would not so much as share a beer with me when we were together during the harvest. Generally, there was an overall coherence between the reports of behavior and the behavior I observed; a good test of that was, I think, in the reactions of other tramps to Carl's remarks and acts. My overriding sense is that tramps not only are unusually self-aware but that they live, by and large, as they say they do.

Carl's work experiences were largely typical of others I've met. While the apple harvest he steered us toward was his first, his other jobs—sheepherding, railroad work, menial labor for individuals or businesses, other fruit work and ranchhanding—are all jobs tramps typically take on. He had been on the road half of his life and said the army made him a tramp. Knowing so little about other paths to the road it is difficult to know whether Carl's early childhood, his father's drinking and desertion of his family, his rejection by his mother, the breakup of his family during the depression and his army life are typical kinds of life patterns for those who hit the road. Undoubtedly they were important parts of Carl's development. When I asked tramps what put a man on the road, most of their answers were deliberately vague, and I do not believe that a systematic investigation of this question could be accomplished.

What may seem an anomoly, Carl's continuing commitment to his mother, turned out to be fairly common among many tramps who maintained fragile family ties. Certainly, Carl's values represented those I found nearly everywhere. Independence was guarded even to the end that it meant one would remain encapsulated and separated from nearly all human connections. One must wonder about the role of women in this life, for I neither saw women nor heard of them aside from an occasional remark about getting laid on a binge. The lack of women did not cause any apparent hardship and the one time I asked Carl about it he did not even take my question seriously. In fact, their lives had an almost puritanical air—constant references to honesty, reputation and hard work, and disgust at those demeaning themselves in front of outsiders or unable to live the tramp life properly. While many lacked Carl's finesse at the life or his understanding of tramp ways and how they had deteriorated, he was by no means unique in his understanding or his ability to express himself. When we first met I noticed his Wellingtons and wondered if he knew what he was doing; by the end of our association I believed that I had been taken along by one who was squarely and completely on the road. My apprenticeship, like the apprenticeship of many anthropologists who be-

144

come members of the groups they study, provided a strong and legitimate way, I believe, to learn what was taken for granted by the rest.

I have tried to write the language as it was spoken. The principal way I did this was to recall conversations by remembering key sentences or phrases. I can literally remember, for example, Blackie telling me of the "prime of his pride," or Jack saying he'd be a "lyin' pig-fucker" if he told us something he didn't know for sure. I think my senses were energized by my desire to remember what I heard, and this was made easier by my enjoyment of the directness with which things are said past the middle border. I carried a small notebook in my shirt pocket and during the hours we waited for trains I often walked away to take notes to help me reconstruct later on. I never wrote in the presence of tramps. I also carried a small tape recorder which I used only to record a few of the conversations, almost all with Carl, late at night. Some of the tramps carry transistor radios, so the tape recorder could have been integrated into what I was doing, but I never felt right relying on mechanical means to mediate the human connection I wished to write about. In that sense the tape recorder was like the camera. I wished to have the most accurate visual and narrative information but I wasn't willing to use these instruments when they would violate the naturalness of the settings. As it happens, the conversations as they are rendered in *Good Company* are the product of four major revisions and many briefer reconsiderations. The general process of recreating the spoken word has been the most difficult part of this project.

Making and Using Photographs

The photographs in this study perform two functions. The first can be thought of as a visual inventory of typical behavior in typical spaces—for this group street corners and sidewalks, alleys, missions, freight yards, places on trains where tramps ride, jungles, and one of many work settings. The photographs portray both tramp life and skid row life. In another essay (Harper 1979) I have analyzed these photographs in terms of things tramps typically say about the situations presented; my intention is to place the viewer more in the position of those in the images—to present the meaning of the images in terms of tramps. In this collection of narrative and images the reader/ viewer is in a position, I believe, to make these connections naturally.

The images are also documents portraying the development of my relations with those I studied. On one level the relations were dependent on the extent to which I was willing to give; whether I went "home" at night; whether I was willing to subject myself and my photographic equipment to the rigors of the life. These issues influenced my choice of equipment. The photograph of the tramp in front of the "Bread of Life Mission" sign, for example, can stand for all photographs made from a perspective of minimal involvement. The photograph was made with a long telephoto lens and a clanking Nikon as I watched unobserved from across the street. If a photograph had been made of me at that moment it would show an individual burdened with two cameras and two accessory lenses draped around his neck, keeping his distance, ready in the late afternoon to retreat to a place quite removed from the setting being photographed. I was working as do photojournalists, and perhaps it is correct to say that the image was "stolen." It is true that I knew nothing of the individual who appears, and my concern for protecting equipment kept me from trying to learn.

As I involved myself more I had to reassess my purpose and methods. I could have continued as I had begun and produced a photographic study from the viewpoint of an outsider, but as I felt myself pulled into the life, my photographic activity changed very much. On the trip I have described I carried a Leica and a single lens—a small, unobtrusive and quiet camera. I made few photographs during my time with Carl. I introduced myself as a writer and photographer and he did not seem to mind my taking pictures until we encountered people he'd known for a long time; then he made it clear that to carry on would be out of the question. Some of the photographs I did make, however, show how the camera may describe the relation between "researcher" and "informant." The image that communicates this best is of Carl handing me a piece of toast. The toast was made at my request. The fire was the first we'd made in days. A long trip was nearly completed and our relationship had the quality of those in which important events have been shared. I am satisfied with the photograph for it describes both an important activ-

146

ity and the nature of our relationship. The photographs I did not take, of Boston Blackie, One-Eyed Jack, and the jungles along the way testify by their absence to the same issue. The relationship between the photographer and subject in a fieldwork experience is very complicated, but for me the rights and desires of the individuals we choose as subjects are more important than a final purpose that would justify making images when they would not be welcomed. The camera must sometimes be left behind.

History and Economy

The men with whom I traveled are part of a way of life which began in the United States after the Civil War. I'd like to briefly describe this tramp history to show how changing material circumstances have affected the life while certain cultural features have continued throughout the period. There are several more detailed tramp histories (Alsop 1967; Bruns 1980) and in another essay I have described the treatment of the tramp in sociological literature (Harper 1976).

In 1923 Nels Anderson wrote that the hobo should be understood as part of the settling of the American frontier. The settlement took place in an entrepreneurial, capitalistic framework. When new regions were exploited for their natural resources or as technological change altered labor needs in extractive or agricultural economies, workers went to the job voluntarily and alone, without intending to settle down. The work was intermittent, corresponding to seasonal agricultural cycles or to the demands of large but one-time building projects. While tramp work varied, all jobs required strength, dexterity and, in some cases, a specialized set of skills. Job sites were primitive and isolated. The tramp expected to set the pace of his work and to remain largely unsupervised, and the bosses knew that their control over the worker as a person was limited and temporary.

A way of life—a culture—grew up in these circumstances. The character of the work, the need for migration, the extreme independence born out of necessity and sometimes a carefully cultivated ability to live without plans or possessions, an outlawry and the roguishness of the hustler, and sprees of drinking in areas called skid roads (named after Pine Street in Seattle, where logs were skidded to the mill and the institutions of the migrant, single man—bars,

147

whorehouses and missions—were located) all came to be known as the way of the hobo, the way of the tramp.

The social and economic situations to which tramp life corresponds exists in three periods. The first extends from the end of the Civil War to roughly the end of the First World War. The characteristics of this period relevant to the history of tramping are industrial development, the closing of the frontier, and the establishing of stable communities based on industrial production and mechanized agriculture. It was during this period that tramps were most numerous, most economically useful, and also seen as most threatening. Many on the road, particularly during economic recessions or depressions, were unsuccessful in finding work, and many were uninterested in work if it was available. Although the definitions vary, there was a popular notion that the hobo was a migratory worker and the tramp a migratory nonworker, and that the bum did not work or travel. Alsop tells us that as late as 1923 there were over a hundred thousand migrants working the grain belt alone (1967, 343), all using the freights for transport. Whole areas of the economy, such as midwestern grain farming or Pacific northwestern lumbering, came to depend on the movement of populations of workers to and from the job as the situation demanded. Yet Hamlin Garland describes these tramp workers as a "flight of alien, unclean birds" descending upon the harvest fields in July, to "vanish into the north in September as mysteriously as they had appeared" (1917, 174). Michael Lesy (1973) tells us that rural and small-town life in the Midwest was dominated by phobias created by social conditions of which tramp bands were a part. Most saw the tramp when he was out of work and hustling to stay alive as he moved to a job, and most during this period considered him an individual on the road because of his personal moral failings. Jack London was an important exception. To London, tramps were social facts, a floating army of surplus labor. The population included both those "less fit and efficient, switchmen who wrecked trains and blacksmiths who lamed horses," and "good men, splendidly skilled and efficient, but thrust out of the employment of dying or disaster-smitten industries" (quoted in Foner 1947, 481). "While it is not nice that these men should die," London concludes, "it is ordained that they must die, and we should not quarrel with them if they cumber our highways and kitchen stoops with their perambulating carcasses. This is a form of

148

elimination we not only countenance but compel. Therefore let us be cheerful and honest about it. Let us be as stringent as we please with our police regulations, but for goodness' sake let us refrain from telling the tramp to go to work. Not only is it unkind, but it is untrue and hypocritical. We know there is no work for him. Or the scapegoat to our economic and industrial sinning, or to the plan of things, if you will we should give him credit. Let us be just. He is so made. Society made him. He did not make himself" (Foner 1947, 487).

An important feature of the 1900–1920 tramp history is the radicalization of the tramp worker by the Industrial Workers of the World. There are several studies of the IWW in general and the participation of the hobo in this movement (Dubofsky 1969; Renshaw 1967; Tyler 1967; DeCaux 1970; St. John 1919; Taft 1960; Facciolo 1977). What is important for my purposes here is the understanding that the political consciousness of the early twentieth century reached the tramp worker, and for a time his zealously guarded independence was set aside for collective and radical political activity. For large numbers the analysis offered by London and other socialist writers was a common-sense interpretation of their experiences. Tramp workers saw their relations to bosses naturally as class war, and devised methods in areawide strikes and free speech movements that were consistent with their way of life. The IWW declined in the late teens and early twenties for several reasons including a gradual acceptance by the working class of industrial capitalism, a xenophobia about communism after the Russian revolution and the opposition by the IWW to the First World War which led to widespread repression by the U.S. government. The effective end of the IWW left the tramp worker without a political voice and seemingly without a political consciousness. I spoke of this history with those I met on the road. Few were interested. The modern tramp eschews any collective political action in order to preserve the independence seen as the cornerstone to the life as it is now lived.

Nels Anderson suggests that the tramp belongs only to the era I have described above: "The true hobo was the in-between worker, willing to go anywhere to take a job and equally willing to move on later. His in-between role related to the two frontiers. He came on the scene after the train blazer, and he went off the scene as the second frontier was closing" (1961, xviii). However, while different economic

149

and social settings have given this way of life a different character tramp culture has persisted.

The 1930s, the era of the great depression, is a second period in the history of the American tramp. While whole areas were uprooted and families often hit the road together, the biographies of Woody Guthrie (1943), W. Z. Foster (1939), Loren Eiseley (1975) and selected sociological studies (Sutherland and Locke 1936; Anderson, 1940b) show that for many this period was a rejuvenation of hobo life. That hobos and tramps from an earlier period lingered on to teach the ways to those new to the road is powerfully told in John Dos Passos' novel *U.S.A.* (1937). Important changes, however, mark the economic and social setting of the depression tramp. There was little work to stimulate migration; most on the road were drifters hustling and begging to stay alive. The availability of automobiles created a new kind of mobility for those just a little better off than the tramp. Unemployment insurance and other social legislation had the effect of keeping many unemployed people at home, and continuing technological development eliminated more forms of tramp work. "The advent of machinery was threatening the grain harvesting jobs. Ice-making machinery would soon replace making ice on the lakes. Soon there would be no more construction of the railroads. On levee work the dredges and drag lines would soon replace the team outfits. Even that favorite winter retreat of migrants, lumbering, was soon to be mechanized" (Anderson 1940a, 12). Yet these social and economic factors did not eliminate the tramp. Tramping became one part of a huge dislocation, an option mostly for men, and those among men who were willing to give up family and place for the open road. Different economic and social factors have influenced the nature of tramp in the current period, extending from the end of the Second World War. The economy has continued to settle down. Work processes have become more rationalized and labor forces have become more stationary. Seasonal work in agriculture that is not done with machines has come to be done by black, Mexican and other immigrant families in what is generally characterized as exploitative work situations. Only in a few isolated economies and on a few railroads does the tramp continue in a manner which connects him to the past I have described.

The apple harvest in the Pacific Northwest is one of the last magnets to draw the hobo worker. The work is similar to earlier tramp

150

work, requiring stamina and dexterity in handling delicate fruit. The work is done alone at a pace and for durations determined by the individual worker. Relations between boss and worker reflect the understanding implicit in earlier work arrangements: nowhere is there the right to crowd a loner—in fact the system works best when both parties leave each other alone. Perhaps the most important similarity to frontier work lies in the willingness of the tramp to appear when the work needs to be done and disappear when the work is completed. Freights continue to provide the means by which this migration takes place and crews are lenient when the workers need to get to the job or leave town. In an overall system that no one publicly acknowledges, the needs of the orchard owners, the fruit pickers and the local economies are all met. The police keep things moving as scheduled by rounding up workers turned eyesores who have lingered too long after the harvest, and put them on the trains themselves.

On those jobs such as ranchhanding, sheepherding and menial labor on the railroads that do not have a strictly seasonal character the tramp behaves similarly. He works hard and leaves when he feels pressured. The pressures may seem minor. One-Eyed Jack left because he was served eggs for breakfast or another tramp did not like the horse he was to sheepherd with. Other examples can be considered more directly exploitative. Carl described being hired to pick grain in the rail yard but being told to do mechanical work which ruined his clothes. Another tramp described having his wage rate changed after the work had begun. Carl quit a job because a labor contractor charged the railroad for the time his workers spent eating but kept the wages himself. Tramps leave jobs in these circumstances because they have no power to bargain for fair treatment, no interest in organizing to gain that power, and because the jobs have no future—there is always another down the line.

While modern tramp work is similar to earlier tramp work, it is also vulnerable to similar economic, technological and social forces. The owner for whom Carl and I worked spoke of the probable introduction of a mechanical apple picker as causing changes reminiscent of those inaugurated by the introduction of the grain harvesting combine in the 1920s. The work would become the management of machines, coordinated in work crews, closely supervised and salaried. Because of all the tramp values in his work experiences, and because of the expectations of foremen in this kind of work, the tramp would not become the tender of the apple-picking machine. This was recognized by our owner, and while he spoke of these changes as nearly inevitable I had the sense he would miss the tramp the way we miss any of the more fully human parts of our life that disappear.

The material base of tramp life is further undermined by changes in the railroad itself. As trains travel faster on deteriorating rails the ride becomes more physically punishing than many can endure. The cars are in a process of being redesigned, as Carl pointed out, so that the nooks and crannies in which the tramp rides are, one by one, eliminated. The ends of the grain cars are built without floors. Piggybacks have only a narrow platform for truck tires, gondolas are covered and boxcars are sealed. These changes are undertaken for reasons that have nothing to do with tramps, yet they inexorably affect a group life which has come to depend upon certain technological designs and forms. Perhaps, then, the end predicted by Anderson is only forestalled. As these material changes continue there will soon be no context into which tramp life may fit.

Although the current social context would be unrecognizable to the tramp of a hundred years ago, I believe that the men with whom I shared the road have more than a superficial similarity to those men who lived the life in the past. The tramp is, in a sense, organic to the American social landscape. American society has always had a fluid character, more fluid than other industrialized countries in Europe and less rigid, of course, than traditional societies in less "developed" areas of the world. England's transition from feudalism to capitalism produced the "sturdy beggar," and many nonwestern societies sanction the wanderer with a religious identity. But in America it has been the nature of the immigration, a national ideology of individualism coming out of a simultaneous land settlement and industrialization, and a lack of a hereditary and conservative (in the way of an aristocracy) ruling class that has made the American tramp persistent. I think these issues have something to do with the ambivalence the public feels toward the tramp: while he represents the threat posed by those who do not take the conventional roles offered by society, he is also somewhat of a hero in his rejection of the routine, regulation and boredom of a life lived in the carefully protected niches of an increasingly organized society.

152

I have mentioned certain expectations tramps have of their work experiences as common throughout their history, and that a certain view of independence remains at the basis of nearly all the tramp does. There are, however, several tramp voices to consider beyond these I've reported.

The dominant theme in tramp tales is that of the tramp as trickster. The tramp invariably gets his last laugh, his free ride after the train crews and police grow weary of the chase, or his free food after the successful hustle. The tramp takes none but his own rules seriously and even those are negotiable. Strawberry, in my reports, even manipulated the local police to take him to and from his jungle for daily supplies of wine and beer. The tramp remains free of and unrepentent to a society which he perceives as a set of pressures to conform, to take orders, and to be unadventuresome. These messages run throughout early biographies (Flynt 1899; Tully 1924; London 1907; Kemp 1920, 1922): they appear in the memoirs of those who lived the tramp life in the thirties (as cited earlier, the work of Guthrie, Foster and Eiseley), they appear as qualities of the hobos encountered in the beat writers Kerouac (1955, 1960), and Cassady (1971), and they permeate nearly everything Carl said to me. The tramp is a trickster both because he is colorful and arrogant, and because he has, compared to what most people naturally expect from the material world, little to lose. When jobs are intermittent and easily replaced, even a jail term for loitering, for a public drunk or for an illegal ride is a temporary stall along the road, and one with regular food.

The tramp world has always required resourcefulness, cunning, persistence and intelligence. These qualities are illustrated in the way tramps use the freights. Tramps have always moved on freights and in particular ways the freight train fits the needs and the personality of the tramp. Trains are difficult to ride, illegal and dangerous. Mastering the trains serves as a selective process where only the most resourceful and keen may survive. More than any other element in the life, the train symbolizes the tramp's self-image. The train poses the immediate possibility of changing one's situation; it offers an arena in which the tramp may prove and reprove himself; and, to speak metaphorically, it represents always a direction away, a release and the possibility of adventure and a reunion with others who belong. While on the train the tramp is arrogant and aloof—the master of a certain universe. The only other possibility of moving from one place to another, hitchhiking, is avoided and looked down upon because it makes the tramp a beggar.

Mastering the trains includes learning how to reduce the mazes of yards to comprehensive systems in which trains can be located, learning to "read" trains to predict their routes, and learning to ride the variety of cars on the train itself. The tramp must learn which yards to avoid; he must learn to identify people in the yards who will provide information and those who will arrest him or banish him from the yards. This knowledge is complex for the situation in the yards changes as yard police enforce trespassing laws inconsistently or according to factors that have more to do with a local harvest than they do with company policy. Others in the yard—yard masters, car knockers, brakemen and engineers—all must be dealt with in certain ways. One does not approach an engineer in the way that one approaches a brakeman, and on some trains one does not approach any of them at all. Mastering the trains thus means learning how to ask questions, as well as learning what questions ought to be asked. Even the way one confronts a trainman and asks a question is culturally defined and must be done correctly. When I began riding I was too polite—brakemen walked away from my fumbling questions and bulls drove me from the yards. As I gained a confidence in using this new language, train people treated me differently and I realized that they used the same encounters to judge the riders. Those who they decide will follow tramp ways may be helped along; the uneasy peace will be maintained for those who suggest by their manner that they won't get themselves hurt or interfere with the trains.

The trains provided me with an important initiation. At the beginning they intimidated me so that I doubted my ability to ride them at all. On my first ride out of Minneapolis on a midnight hotshot I nearly did myself in with imagined horrors. As I gained miles and experience I grew to feel a strong bond with the freights although they abused me more than had anything in my life. There is something in the relationship between a human being and this particular machine that, I believe, makes the tramp. I never felt as though I was in the life until I'd

154

begun a freight ride, and those I met on the road gave me the impression that the sharing of the ride made up for much that separated us in background and life experience.

Finally, the road breeds a survival instinct which is consistent with the individualism the tramp prizes so highly. I recall Carl's comments after we had been out a few days and many hundreds of miles—the train slowed as it paralleled a highway and we watched a Winnebago travel trailer just a few yards away keeping pace with our boxcar. Carl spoke for all tramps when he said: "Would you like to live like that? They're afraid to sleep on the ground; they'd turn up their noses at the perfectly good food we've been eating—they live for those things and they can't live without them." This kind of independence means both the ability to live with few possessions and it means defining oneself apart from the material things people surround themselves with. The ability to go without must be seen as more than a rationalization for the failure to possess in a way that is normally taken for granted. There was utter confidence in Carl's plans to travel a few thousand miles to new work with a dollar and some change, and he had enough sense to bring along the things he needed to make the trip manageable. The trip was not a desperate gesture by a confused alcoholic although the decisions to leave were made at the end of a three-week drunk. And while there were mistakes—Carl missed his hotshot and had to buy ready-made cigarettes—his survival was never in question. He prided himself in his knowledge of geographies and economies that enabled him, either legally or illegally, to get his food. It is probably these skills which make the tramp, in his own eyes, free. It may be easy to idealize or overemphasize this quality in the life. But on the other hand tramps exist without most of the props we put between ourselves and our environments, and they laugh at the ends we go to maintain them. I found extremely disconcerting the realization that most of my plans and accommodations were socially constructed and could be easily left behind, and I admired the way the tramps live more directly, more immediately, and with fewer rationalizations. John McCook, who studied the hobo nearly eighty years ago, communicated this sense:

> The average man grows up to live a regular life and to work as a part of it. We are taught to believe that there is a necessary relation between doing our daily tasks, eating our regular meals, going to bed in a fixed place,

rising at a pre-arranged hour, wearing a certain kind of clothes, that there is between all this and being "good" an unalterable relationship: as also between being good and being happy. Religion gives its awful sanction to this theory, habit fortifies it; successive generations of what we call civilization even create an instinct which even makes us think, or at least say, we like it: When suddenly to one of us comes the discovery that we can stop all this and yet live—nay, grow fat, perhaps, and vigorous and strong; drop worry and responsibility . . . go everywhere, see everything . . . and when that discovery comes, it is apt to be fatal. (Quoted in Bruns 1980, 74)

There is also a dark side. Tramp life began and remains violent. The violence comes from the culture, from those who ride "to pick the pickers," and from without, from police, train crews and vigilante groups. If we are to believe the tramp biographies, there was much more violence from train police in the past. Jack London described in eighteen pages the efforts of a train crew to ditch him on one ride (they failed), and literally thousands died as a result of these chases. Now one hears that in the Burlington Northern yards in Chicago the police shoot at trespassers, but being arrested for riding now seems to have more to do with where and when and how a rider makes his way. If you ride through Texas during the pea harvest, say the tramps, ride carefully or you'll pick peas for the state for a month and a half. There are bulls in particular yards, and whole lines, such as the Union Pacific, where police are serious. But usually, if you learn how to ride as a tramp, as I've suggested above, you will be left alone. The violence comes from the uncertain group that used the trains, and from tramps themselves. The first tramp I met in a boxcar pulled a gun on me when I tried to make friendly conversation. He told me he'd been robbed for the last time. Another, as we approached on the Seattle skid row, turned and pulled a rusty knife which he quickly put to my friend's throat. I was once waiting in a boxcar in the Seattle yards with five or six others when the police came by to warn us of two "armed and dangerous" escaped convicts who had ditched their stolen car at the edge of the yard. A few minutes later the train began to leave and two desperado types, with no gear, jumped into the car. I'd been waiting all day for the train and decided to stay, but violence smoldered in the background. Halfway into a seven-mile tunnel—total blackness, thunderous noise and suffocating dirt and diesel fumes—I heard a black tramp who weighed at least 280 pounds cry out like a child: "Don't touch me!" I waited, trying to brace myself on something as I sat with my back against the wall near the door, but nothing happened. The train passed back into the night and the boxcar seemed like a cage filled with wild animals who were equally able to do each other in. I jumped the first time the train slowed, but the rest, more able than I in that arena, stayed behind to take their chances.

But perhaps the greatest contradiction between ideal and experience lies in the use of alcohol. Tramps may see themselves as the last of the independents, but they lose it often when they drink. Many maintain a precarious balance and lose it only occasionally; some lose it altogether and end up "a hollow shell on skid row with nothing but the clothes on their backs." The irony is that alcohol provides the release and much of the sociability and yet, at the same time, the most awful form of bondage.

The release is often social drinking—drinking with others who live the same life. When I mentioned that I liked to drink with my friends, Carl pointed out:

> "You're just like some of us—you can't find your friends but in a barroom."
> "We aren't in a barroom," I answered.
> "That's because we can't afford it. Where else are you going to meet your buddies . . . Are you going to meet them in church? You can't talk like they do in church. You going to meet them in a poolroom? There ain't no more good poolrooms! So where else is there to meet?"
> "Well, if you got a house, if you have a place . . ."
> "If you got a house. We haven't got houses. We got a bedroll, so we get together around a jungle, a fire, and bullshit. And then, if we meet each other in a tavern we bullshit, but then we drink, too!"

This kind of drinking is probably most extreme among tramps who work long periods by themselves, such as sheepherders or prospectors. When large stakes are spent, everyone—bartenders, buddies, jackrollers and police—take their cuts. These episodes probably have a great deal to do with releasing the energy built up in long periods of isolation, and can be understood as temporary excursions out of the routine. Many, however, as Carl, drink alone and in what appear to be regular patterns.

Carl described drinking sessions that ranged from planned "vacations" to unplanned binges. Realizing the difficulty in making this contradictory and partly inconsistent reality into discrete categories, I will suggest that these two extremes represent types of drunks in which the essential difference is the amount of control exercised by the drinker.

In what I shall call the planned drunk (Carl did not use this term) Carl drank at a rate which would keep him drunk but not incapacitated. Carl told of drinking three quarts of whiskey a day (keeping "aglow" but not unconscious for long periods), staying in a hotel (one can imagine an old hotel of faded elegance at the edge of a skid row), had himself shaved and manicured every day, and generously tipped the waitress in the hotel bar where he drank alone for hours. The appeal of this role reversal is obvious. When it became routine the drunk was finished. Carl said simply: "I stop when I get bored, hell, I wasn't doing anything!" This kind of a drunk uses up money accumulated during periods of work, and if we accept that the tramp does not seek to surround himself with pieces of the world he has purchased, the planned drunk, the vacation, seems a reasonable event in a normal round of working, drinking, and moving to a new situation.

On a binge, an "unplanned drunk" however, the drinker is nearly out of control. Carl drank in the open, became filthy, was robbed and hurt, and used money he had planned for other things. It is the binge that may become extended indefinitely and lead the tramp to a permanent life on skid row. But even the binge as described by Carl, Blackie and others has a natural life which ends with the depletion of honorably gained money. The tramp may borrow money from a liquor store owner or another tramp, or bum an "eye-opener" from a bartender, but he will not beg on the streets to stay drunk. On the skid rows are those who have lost this essential control, and at times tramps are there with them. The groups overlap but they are not the same. Studies of skid row life are not studies of the tramp.

Even this kind of binge is accepted and laughed at as long as the tramp keeps a certain amount of control. Carl and Blackie told mournful tales about drunks and lost jobs and ill-spent money, and Blackie finally concluded: "Several times lately I found myself wondering—just what the hell's going to become of me?" and they both laughed until they nearly fell on the ground. These attitudes were consistent from tramp to tramp, related to the more basic commitment tramps maintain not to sink to the level of the bum. These ideas explain the aversion Carl, and others, felt in the presence of those who drank in ways tramps would not. Carl called them riffraff. Not only did they drink at the wrong times and in the wrong ways, but they wore the wrong clothes, and rode freights incorrectly. The relationship between the tramps and the riffraff was shown when, in a boxcar with nearly forty men, two gallons of Thunderbird wine were passed around, I sensed the pull of the wine—the day was hot and the wine cool—but only a few joined the bottle gang. Carl later pointed out that they wore "three-quarter height shoes with white socks falling over their ankles, clothes that looked like they had come out of a Salvation Army barrel, and they didn't have hats to cover their filthy hair." They even rode incorrectly. They stayed near the door and some sat with their feet hanging over the side, as if to tempt a close sign or a switchman's marker. Their noise and carousing were out of character with the quiet and wary presence of the others who were uncomfortable and nervous packed so tightly in the car. For the rest the bottle would wait.

Finally, I think the issue of control may be easily overemphasized. To consider drinking, whether planned or unplanned, as essentially a way to use up capital accumulated because the tramp works so hard, is incomplete. While I believe that it is possible to be a tramp and not drink, for nearly all I met alcohol was reported to have caused major problems. But in the balance I was left with a strong sense that the tramp understands, and usually accepts, his imperfectly realized life. Carl chided himself for getting his life out of order—drinking when he should have been working, but then he laughed:

"Now I save penny, penny, penny; when I drink it's dollars, dollars, dollars!" and finally he concluded that to second guess himself, to relive his decisions, would accomplish nothing.

The tramp may accept his drinking, but in another perspective it victimizes him while it benefits specific groups in the areas where he drinks. His wages end up in the coffers of the bars or the police, or in the pockets of jackrollers. If all were well it could be said that the system is in quiet balance, but as it is, the tramp is more like a catalyst in a set of economic changes. He may be used in a number of ways but in the end he gains little. Ironically, that may be what he desires most.

159

The ethic of independence that underscores all of these values is not without its own costs. Tramps speak of and act within a true communalism, yet when things really become difficult the tramp takes care of himself and leaves the others behind. While "freedom" and "independence" are easily defended on philosophical grounds, in the tramp world these values keep people from any relationship which requires a serious commitment. My perspective as I write final revisions at age thirty-two is different from the perspective in which I experienced these things in my mid-twenties. Perhaps with family, house and job I am more realistic or perhaps I have simply accommodated myself as tramps suggest most do. I'm more confused; the benefits, the joys of this accommodation are in the laughter of my children but I see as well the loss of choice in my daily life. Tramp lessons can be thought of as a sick evaluation of ego concerns, but they represent in a particular way the truest voice I've heard telling me I must face personally and alone the implications of my decisions.

Earlier I described technological change which threatens the life. Other changes threaten as well. There are few left; the culture seems to lack a "critical mass"—sufficient numbers to keep something historically coherent alive. While real tramps may be few in number, nontramp riders use the trains without regard for the implicit understanding between riders and yardmen. They break the seals of loaded boxcars and sometimes leave with the contents, they break into new cars on auto carriers, ride with women and animals; they hang their feet out of boxcar doors and show off going through towns. They violate the quality of invisibility which the tramp cultivates and which keeps him out of trouble. Others drink in the yard and get run over by boxcars as they lie drunk on the rails at night or they drink and fall out along the way. These accidents cause trouble for the railroads; they are inconvenient, and because the railroads are legally liable they represent the possibility of serious lawsuits. These changes have coincided with a change in the yardmen themselves. Old brakemen may have seen a bit of the road themselves and they helped us along. Younger yardmen were less likely even to speak to us and they often treated us as though we were soiling their trains and yards.

All of this takes place as the old ways are forgotten by those few who are left. Jungles were once left clean, and with a mirror in the tree and a pile of wood waiting to be used. Now these practices are part of the memories of a few who have spent most of their years on the road. Even the words they use to describe the life as it had been lose their meaning. When Carl said "the oldtimer, the real tramp—he'd have nothing to do with this bunch," he expressed shame over how bad it had become. Soon even those few will be gone and memories will blink out, one by one.

Bibliography

Alsop, Kenneth. 1967. *Hard Travelin': The Hobo and His History*. New York: New American Library.

Anderson, Nels. 1923, 1961. *The Hobo: The Sociology of the Homeless Man*. Chicago: University of Chicago Press. (Phoenix edition, with new Introduction, 1961.)

———. 1940a. *Men On the Move*. Chicago: University of Chicago Press, 1940.

———. 1940b. "Highlights of the Migrant Problem Today." *Proceedings of the National Conference of Social Work* 67: 109–17.

Bruns, Roger. 1980. *Knights of the Road: A Hobo History*. New York: Methuen.

Cassady, Neal. 1971. *The First Third*. San Francisco: City Lights Books.

DeCaux, Len. 1970. *Labor Radical: From the Wobblies to CIO*. Boston: Beacon Press.

Dubovsky, Melvin. 1969. *We Shall Be All*. New York: Quadrangle.

Eiseley, Loren. 1975. *All the Strange Hours: The Excavation of a Life*. New York: Charles Scribner's Sons.

Facciolo, Jay. 1977. "The Wobs and the Bos: The IWW and the Hobo." Master's thesis, Hunter College.

Feied, Frederick. 1964. *No Pie in the Sky: The Hobo as American Cultural Hero*. New York: Citadel Press.

Foner, Philip. 1947. *Jack London: American Rebel*. New York: Citadel Press.

Foster, William Z. 1939. *Pages From a Worker's Life*. New York: International Publishers Co.

Flynt, Josiah. 1899. *Tramping with Tramps: Studies and Sketches of Vagabond Life*. New York: The Century Company.

Garland, Hamlin. 1917. *A Son of the Middle Border*. New York: Macmillan Company.

Guthrie, Woody. 1943. *Bound for Glory*. New York: New American Library.

Harper, Douglas. 1976. *The Homeless Man: An Ethnography of Work,*

Trains and Booze. Ph.D. Diss. Ann Arbor, Mich.: University Microfilms.

———. 1979. "Life on the Road." in Wagner, Jon, ed., *Images of Information.* Beverly Hills: Sage Publications.

Hughes, Everett. 1971. *The Sociological Eye.* Chicago: Aldine.

Jay, Robert. 1972. "Personal and Extra Personal Vision in Anthropology." In *Reinventing Anthropology,* edited by Del Hymes. New York: Random House.

Kemp, Harry. 1920. *Canteys and Ballads.* New York: Brentanos.

———. 1922. *Tramping on Life.* Garden City, N.J.: Garden City Publishing Co.

Kerouac, Jack. 1955. *On the Road.* New York: Viking Press.

———. 1960. *Lonesome Traveler.* New York: McGraw-Hill.

Lesy, Michael. 1973. *Wisconsin Death Trip.* New York: Random House.

London, Jack. 1907. *The Road.* New York: Macmillan Company.

Renshaw, Patrick. 1967. *Wobblies. The Story of Syndicalism in the United States.* New York: Doubleday.

St. John, Vincent. 1919. *The I.W.W.* Chicago: I.W.W.

Spradley, James P. 1970. *You Owe Yourself a Drink: An Ethnography of Urban Nomads.* Boston: Little Brown and Company.

Sutherland, Edwin H., and Harvey J. Locke. 1936. *Twenty Thousand Homeless Men.* Chicago: J. P. Lippincott Company.

Taft, Philip. 1960. "The I.W.W. in the Grain Belt." *Labor History* 1 (Winter): 53–67.

Tully, Jim. 1924. *Beggars of Life: A Hobo Autobiography.* New York: Random House.

Tyler, Robert L. 1967. *Rebels of the Woods: The IWW in the Pacific Northwest.* Eugene: University of Oregon Books.

164

Glossary

Airdale	A tramp who is an extreme loner.
Apple knocker	An apple-picking tramp
Badorder	A wrecked boxcar on its way to the repair yard
Bindle stiff	A tramp who carries all his gear in burlap gunny sacks; also used to refer to old-fashioned tramps
B.N.	Burlington Northern
Boxcar tramp	A tramp who regularly rides boxcars
Braky	Brakeman
Bull	Railroad police
Bull local	A freight which travels between divisions, often stopping at local yards
Bum	A skid row alcoholic, found infrequently on freight trains. Does not work, stays drunk, usually drinks wine
Car knocker	A yard man who works assembling trains
Catch	To board the train
Catch back	To ride the way you have come on a freight
Catch him on the run	To board the train when it is moving
Crummy	Caboose
Division	Main freight yards, usually five hundred miles apart. Through freights stop only at divisions. Also called "five-hundred milers"
Drag line	The track onto which a train is pulled when being passed on the main line
Empty	An empty boxcar; a boxcar without a load. A boxcar with tramps in it is still an empty

Flat	Flat car
Flat-wheeler	A bad-riding car, or an old fashioned boxcar with "hotbox" axles instead of those equipped with Timkin roller bearings
Flop	Noun, meaning a place to sleep (e.g., "I took a flop") or verb (e.g., "I'll flop here")
Gandy dancer	A railroad worker
G.N.	Great Northern
Go junking	To scavenge for scrap metal or other material to sell for salvage
Gondola	A shallow, uncovered car
Grab iron	A bar welded onto a boxcar over the couplings which can be used to hold on to when jumping over the couplings
Head end	The front section of the train
Helpers	Extra engines usually attached to the middle of the train to pull it over an upgrade
Highball	To go full speed
Highball Whistle	One short and one long whistle, means the train is about to be underway
High line	The old Great Northern route through the Dakotas, Montana, Idaho and Washington
High line hotshot	The "through" freight on the high line
High-roller	Originally a gambling term. Means a hustling tramp, a particular style of acting
Hobo	A wandering man who works infrequently but is not a bum; a historical term, used infrequently today. Nels Anderson, in *The Hobo* (1923), discussed an explicit stratification of social structure with categories called hobos, tramps, bums, etc. In many ways the stratification is still similar, although the lines have broken down considerably, and the term hobo has fallen to misuse. Also called 'bo

Homeguard	A tramp who does not travel
Hot	(a) Illegal and dangerous. (b) Fast
Hot boxes	Old-style lubrication on boxcar axles. Boxcars with hot boxes are rough riding
Hotshot	A freight train which goes cross country without breaking up, except for minor reshufflings at major divisions
Hot yard	A freight yard where tramps are arrested for riding
Hump	(a) A small, man-made hill in a yard over which uncoupled cars are pushed. A single track over the hill spreads into many tracks. Cars are reshuffled as a trainman in a tower switches the cars from one order to another. (b) The continental divide. Riding over the "hump" is a trip over the Rockies
Jungle	(a) A tramp camp, usually with grill and seats, sometimes with mirror, wood supply and cooking cans; (b) a social group that regularly occupies a camp; (c) as verb, to camp together
Made	The train is "made"—assembled
Main line	The track in the yard on which the through trains run
Mission stiff	A tramp who lives in a mission. Also called a "nose diver"
N.P.	Northern Pacific
Outside 'bo	A tramp who winters outside
Outside ride	Riding a freight car exposed to the elements
Piggyback	A flat car on which a truck-trailer is bolted
Power	Engines. Also called "units"
Ready-mades	Store-bought cigarettes
Reefer	Refrigerator car

Riding bulls	Railroad police who ride on the trains to arrest riders after the train has left the main yard
Round nose	An old Great Northern engine, rounded in front with a single light
Rubber tramp	A tramp who lives and travels in an old automobile
Sally	Salvation Army
Set off	Leave part of the train behind
S.P.	Southern Pacific
S.P. & S.	Spokane, Portland and Seattle Railroad
Square nose	Modern yard engine, angled front end
Tail end	The end of a train
Through freight	Like a hotshot, a freight that goes from division to division without breaking up. Also called a time freight
Tramp	A man on the road. Works, drinks and migrates
Units	Engines
U.P.	Union Pacific Railroad Co.
Up-on-top ride	Riding on top of a boxcar
Whistle stop	A stop in a division to change crews. Takes about twenty minutes
Wino	Generally a bum; low-class tramp
Wintering	Getting by in the winter
Working stiff	A tramp who regularly works
Yard bull	Railroad police who stay in the yards
Yard donkey	Yard engine used to push segments of trains from one track to another
Yard master	Railroad employee who supervises the yard activity

Afterword

Howard S. Becker

Academic social science has so committed itself to objectivity and rigorous measurement that it has lost sight of the complementary virtues of subjective involvement (of both the makers and the consumers of scientific work) and rigorous observation. Participants in that scientific culture may therefore not allow themselves to experience the pleasure and make full use of the knowledge contained in *Good Company*. If this book needs a word of explanation, it is to those who might, on some grounds of scientific ascetism, deny themselves its substantial rewards.

Scientific work relies on subjectivity at many crucial points. The confessional and autobiographical literature of the natural sciences, as well as the social sciences, contains much testimony on the matter. This is, of course, particularly true in the sciences which study human beings, their experiences, and their forms of collective activity. We cannot develop ideas about how and why people do what they do without imagining ourselves in their place and imagining what they might be thinking and experiencing. Even such formalized models as those of economics do that, imputing to economic actors the motives of a rational calculator. Developing ideas worth putting to the rigorous tests of empirical research depends on having subjective experiences sufficiently broad to allow us to capture the state of mind of those whose behavior our theories are supposed to explain. If our subjectivity fails to take account of what those people really are thinking about and the perspectives they jointly bring to bear on their collective activity, then our theories will omit relevant variables and our conclusions will not, to use that language, explain much of the variance we are interested in. The world, in that way, punishes scientists who ignore subjectivity and, as Herbert Blumer has often pointed out, thus substitute their own subjectivity for that of the people studied.

Similarly, people who read and use scientific research results read into even the most objective and dehumanized tables and numerical coefficients a subjective understanding of what those results "mean," what they represent in the actions and feelings of people doing something together. How well readers do that—how well what they read into a research report coincides with what the people they are having these fantasies about actually think and experience—depends on the quality of the information the report gives them. Readers necessarily make do with what they have available. Research reports vary considerably in how much information they give readers (especially on the subjective meaning of events), depending on the conventions of their genre. Surveys typically give tabular summaries, leaving to our imaginations the particular answers and real people who stand behind those numbers. Ethnographic research typically gives selected quotations from field observations, designed to illustrate the larger body of materials which give the report's conclusions their warrant; it is left to readers to imagine the full narrative and social context these snippets come from. Almost every variety of social science reporting leaves to our imaginations what the people and places described actually looked like.

To collect the information that allows the subjective side of life to be taken into account, researchers must engage in rigorous detailed observation. They cannot be satisfied with hearing about events secondhand. They cannot accept statements about "how we usually do things" without seeing for themselves, over a large enough number of occasions, that that *is* how things are done. They ask participants in the events they witness and take part in to describe what is going to happen and what has just happened, so that they can use outside testimony as well as their own experience to understand the meanings others are assigning to those same events. They use their own experiences—the things they do, the things they don't do, the feelings that accompany their own participation—to generate hypotheses about what others are experiencing, hypotheses they can then test in further observation and interviewing in the field. That triangulation of meanings provides a check, for researchers and readers, on haphazard and inaccurate assignments of meaning.

Researchers who conduct that kind of rigorous observation pay a heavy price for it, both personally and scientifically. They spend enormous amounts of time gathering and recording data, often in places far from home and at inconvenient hours. Researchers intent on this kind of accuracy must, further, expose themselves personally to all kinds of people and situations; they cannot hide behind a lab coat or a clipboard and expect to get at the subjective aspects of the worlds they study. That so few social scientists will pay such a price partly accounts for the low state of observation which plagues the social sciences.

The scientific price is the difficulty of accumulating information on large numbers of cases, so that methods of analysis and kinds of generalizations which require large numbers are not available. That makes the resulting research reports vulnerable to criticisms from those who take those methods and forms of generalizations to be the only suitable ones.

Suppose that someone has done the kind of intensive observation required to analyze both the objective and subjective aspects of some social phenomenon adequately. How can that knowledge be presented so that readers can know what the author knows? Experiments that are available in oral history, in the life history materials gathered by anthropologists and sociologists and in their occasional photographic works, suggest some ways. But social scientists have generally had trouble devising adequate formats for the presentation of such knowledge.

Good Company is an enormously successful experiment in gathering and presenting material that gives us a sound and exciting understanding of an otherwise almost inaccessible social world. I cannot improve on Harper's description and analysis of either that world or the way his study contributes to our understanding of larger issues surrounding it. Nor can I improve on his explanation of how the highly personal material the book contains in fact constitutes adequate proof for the more general propositions it suggests.

What remains to be said is that *Good Company* provides an exemplar—in just the sense Thomas Kuhn meant it—of how this kind of knowledge might be presented so that the presentation contains what the researchers came to know in such a way that the reader can share the knowledge. The first-person narrative creates a document of a high degree of authenticity. Harper's photographs make compelling visual images that answer still more questions we might have about the circumstances he describes. (The role of visual materials in the presentation of social science research is another underdeveloped area of thinking.) In both verbal and visual realms the book is a worthy successor to the classic works of "Chicago" sociology, a tradition which has provided a parade of exemplars in which *Good Company* now takes its place.